# The Collegium Maius

## History · Customs · Collections

Karol Estreicher

# THE COLLEGIUM MAIUS

*of the Jagiellonian University*
*in Cracow*

*History · Customs · Collections*

*Interpress Publishers*
*Warsaw 1973*

# TABLE OF CONTENTS

The Jagiellonian University in the 14th century

## Part One • History

## Part Two • Customs

## Part three • Collections

# THE JAGIELLONIAN UNIVERSITY IN THE 14TH CENTURY

The foundation of universities in Central Europe in the 14th century accompanied the general rise in the cultural level of European nations and the emergence of a system of government which called for experts with a knowledge of law. In 1348, Charles IV, King of Bohemia and German Emperor founded a *studium generale* or university in Prague, thus showing the way, as it were, to the neighbouring countries of Germany, Austria, Hungary and Poland. Following the Czech example, the Polish king Casimir the Great, a truly enlightened ruler whose peaceful policies brought Poland out of the darkness of the Middle Ages into the modern era, established a university in Cracow in the year 1364. The 15th-century Polish historian Jan Długosz gives the following account of it:

"King Casimir, wishing to elevate and adorn his kingdom with a *studium generale,* began to build a new university in Kazimierz near Cracow, on a vast site extending over a thousand paces, with fine houses, rooms, lectoria and numerous lodgings for the professors and masters of the new school. Having then dispatched a mission to Pope Urban V in Avignon, he obtained from the Holy See a confirmation of this foundation. Yet after the death of King Casimir (1370), the University suffered a reverse of fortune."

In the Middle Ages, the situation of Cracow, then Poland's capital, was particularly advantageous. The city lay on the important East-West trade routes, on the river Vistula which was navigable almost from its source down to the Baltic Sea.

Receipts from the sales of salt from the huge salt-mine at Wieliczka belonging to the Royal Treasury, the incomes of merchants importing wine from Hungary, and profits from the Eastbound cloth trade, all added to the wealth of the city. Not only the royal residence on the Wawel hill but its economic growth too, made of Cracow a European capital that proved more and more attractive to foreigners. This was also reflected in the lively religious and political life. Thus, if the *studium generale* of University founded in the 14th century survived the critical first period of its existence, this was mainly thanks to the fact that it had been established in a city with a great future.

1364 was an especially fortunate year for Cracow. Numerous European rulers met in Poland's capital on the occasion of the peace concluded between the Emperor Charles IV and Louis of Hungary, with King Casimir acting as mediator. Charles IV arrived with a large retinue. In addition to King Louis, there were King Valdemar of Denmark and King Peter of Cyprus as well as ten other princes. It was a truly magnificent gathering and the memory of it has survived in Cracow to this day in legends and place-names (the Danish Tower at the Castle).

In April 1364, King Casimir wrote to Pope Urban V, then residing in Avignon, with the request that "there might be inaugurated in Cracow, the capital of the Kingdom, a *studium generale* which would, in particular, have faculties of canon and civil law, in view of the great distance of other studia which are more than a 40 days' journey away, so that science is banished from Cracow". Urban V gave his consent and the foundation charter of the University was issued in Cracow on 12 May 1364. Expressing the desire that a "brilliant pearl of learning" should exist in Cracow, the King at the same time conferred a number of privileges on the Rector, professors and students; for instance he granted exemption from customs duties to those arriving to study, assigned lodgings to all those connected with the University, and allotted lucrative salaries which came for the most part from the salt-mines in near-by Wieliczka. While granting privileges and freedoms to the students, the King requested at the same time that the City Council should look after order and discipline among them "so that they may not with impunity roam the streets; those caught doing so should be turned over

to the Rector for judgement and if found guilty, should be expelled from Cracow".
Among historians of the University there has been a longstanding dispute as to where the university founded by Casimir in 1364 was situated. Some — like Brandowski (1864), Krzyżanowski (1900) and Barycz (1951) — assert that the university was located in a suburb of Cracow named Kazimierz after the King; other scholars (e.g. Dąbrowski) maintain that this was out of the question and that the King only started the construction of a building but failed to complete it. According to some sources the university was originally housed in the Wawel Castle (in castro Cracoviensi, 1367). To Dąbrowski's convincing arguments let us only add what we know from King Casimir's charter, namely that in the 14th century the Arts Faculty had its seat in Cracow, in the School of Our Lady, near the Dominican monastery. In any case, medieval universities at first did without buildings of their own since there were few students and not many doctors, or, in other words, professors.

Two other Universities in Central Europe were established almost at the same time as in Cracow: in Vienna (1365) and in Pecs, Hungary (1367). In Germany, universities were founded in Heidelberg (1386), Cologne (1388) and Erfurt (1392). The Universities of Cracow and Vienna based themselves on the Italian model, by which the Rector was elected by the students, but did not have theological faculties which were considered of prime importance at that time.

In spite of many difficulties the Casimir University did survive, for it seems that in the year 1369 the same King Casimir ordered that students be punished for vagrancy at night. At the same time there are references in the city records to bachelors of arts whose degree was conferred on them in Cracow and students "in Universitate studii generalis". Thus, without having a suitable building, the University did function, and contained both masters and students. All in all, we know of some ten sources bearing witness to the activity of the university in Cracow.

What was taught at this oldest University of King Casimir? Lacking the Pope's permission there was no theology but canon and civil law were both taught, based mainly on the 12th-century Collection of *Ecclesiastical Laws by Gratianus* and the *Decretalia* (assembled in the 13th-century by the order of Pope Gregory IX). A third professor lectured on later additions and on Pope Clement V's decrees of 1313 and 1317 (the *Nova Iura*). At the same time, Roman law was taught, based on Justinian's Code, of 533, by a total of eight senior and junior professors. In the medical faculty, two masters taught the medicine of the epoch which probably included the strict interpretation of classical writers and their medical theories. We may assume that these teachers were the same royal physicians who had tried unsuccessfully to cure King Casimir in 1370, i.e. doctors Heinrich from Cologne, Mateusz from Stachów and Mikołaj Polak. The faculty of Arts (philosophy) was located in the School of the Church of Our Lady in the Little Market Square. There one or two masters taught the principles of medieval philosophy according to Aristotle, hammering Latin theses and formulae into the students' heads.

This 14th-century university did not develop successfully; its organization was complex and it lacked adequate equipment. Reforms therefore seemed indicated.

*Collegium Maius*

*History*

A DESCRIPTION • THE BEGINNINGS OF THE COLLEGIUM MAIUS • THE JAGIELLONIAN FOUNDATION • FURTHER EXTENSIONS • ALBERTI'S THEORY • HUMANISM IN THE ARCHITECTURE OF THE COLLEGIUM MAIUS • THE COURTYARD AND GALLERIES • THE CONSTRUCTION OF THE ASSEMBLY HALL AND THE GABLED ROOF • THE LIBRARIA • FURTHER HISTORY OF THE COLLEGIUM • THE PSEUDO-GOTHIC • RESTORATION IN THE 20TH CENTURY

## COLLEGIUM MAIUS —
## A DESCRIPTION

The building of the Collegium Maius in Cracow, acquired its present form, in the course of the 15th century when several houses were joined into one. The entire site extends over 2,587 sq. m.

The Collegium is a three-storeyed building at the corner of St. Anne's and Jagiellońska Streets. Seen from outside are the high windows of the assembly hall, the window-gratings of the so-called residence or professors' lodgings, the windows of the common room (Stuba Communis) and, finally, the windows of the library (Libraria). The simple austere walls are surmounted by three Gothic gables from the late 15th and early 16th century.

A particularly attractive element of the Jagiellońska Street façade is the oriel window of the Common Room, crowned by a little baroque roof.

The courtyard is arcaded and paved with flagstones. In the centre is a well about which Professor Sebastian Petrycy taking Horace as his model wrote as follows in 1609 :

*Who ever will sing your praises,*
*Charming well of the Academy in the*
*building-up Cracow :*

*You were first installed by King Jagiełło,*
*Placed in the centre of the House*
*of Wisdom.*

*Your water as clear as a glass vessel*
*Is worthy to be mixed with sweet wine ;*

In the Middle Ages University buildings were given Latin names. The word Collegium recalls the community of scholars once residing in this building

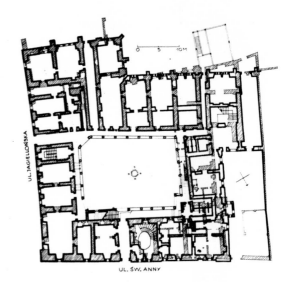

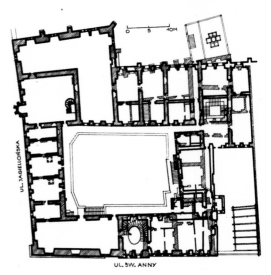

This aerial view of the Collegium shows the building's rectangular plan, and quiet central courtyard

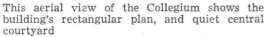

*Long ago you would have borne*
*plentiful flowers*

*Had not the ground been trodden by*
*many a foot.*

*Among all the wells that are to be found*
*In this Polish land of ours, you are*
*the most famous...*

The present marble well was reconstructed in 1958 after the model of similar

The plans of the ground floor and of the two upper floors show the layout and function of the building. Shaded outlines in black show the present walls after reconstruction in the 19th and 20th centuries; double lines indicate the parts demolished in the 19th century

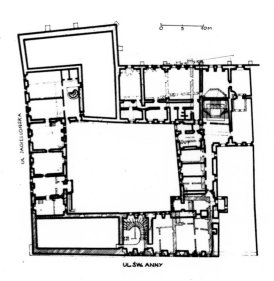

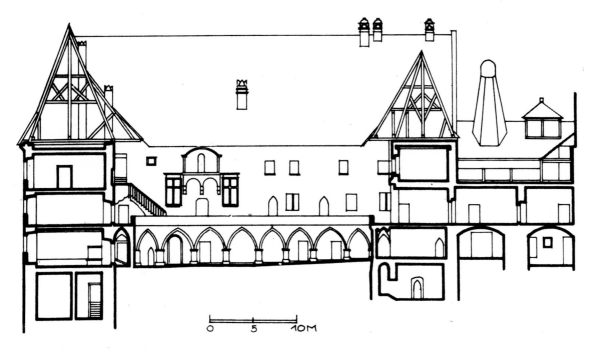

A north-south section of the Collegium Maius shows the state of the building before 1840. To gain more space for the library, the professors' lodgings on the 1st floor were at that time converted into store-rooms and a new storey was added to the kitchen, whose high chimney can be seen over the lower wing

Cracow wells. It is adorned by the coats of arms of Poland and of Cracow, of King Ladislas Jagiełło and his wife Queen Jadwiga of the Anjou dynasty.

Placed under the courtyard arcades and in the gallery are stone sculptures and fragments of architectural ornaments from University buildings. Among the finest is the plaque of the Jerusalem dormitory founded by Cardinal Zbigniew Oleśnicki in the middle of the 15th century.

From the arcades wide stairs known as the Professors' Stairs lead to the first floor thus providing a connection with the gallery. On the left is the entrance to the former assembly hall, also called the Jagiellonian Room. On the opposite side, a sculptured portal leads into the large library, next to which is the common room.

Mention should also be made of the steep roofs over the courtyard from which cascades of water fall down when pouring rain comes, the painted rose ceiling under the roof as well as the various chimneys and weather-vanes rising over the Collegium.

Next to the Collegium is the garden, which is, unfortunately, too overpowered by the neo-Gothic college built in 1900 for the department of physics, and now used by the University's Historical Institute.

Between the Collegium Maius and the Nowodworski College we see (from No. 10 St. Anne's Street) a narrow courtyard which since the Middle Ages has been known as the Foundry. In the background is the house, a wooden porch and an oriel window. The façade of the house is adorned by a Renaissance portal from the former Dormitory of the Poor.

The Collegium Maius is not just a museum to be visited by tourists but is still used by the University for research and teaching and for the sessions of the academic Senate as well as other scholarly meetings. Lectures for students from other institutions of higher learning and drawing lessons are also conducted there. The History of Art Institute has its premises on the second floor where future museum staff and art restorers are trained. The Institute has a modern, beautifully furnished library, open both to students and professors as well as to all interested in research.

The Collegium Maius is open at all times to Polish and foreign visitors, except

The eastern façade of the Collegium Maius seen from the corner of Jagiellońska and St. Anne's streets. The picture shows the oldest part of the Collegium, i.e. the 14th-century corner house which was given to the University in 1400. The original construction of rough-hewn stone and the large hall on the 1st floor, then called palatium, and now used as the University assembly hall have survived unchanged

This buttress of stone blocks, dating from the 18th century, reinforced the walls of the Collegium. Chains on the corners of Cracow houses, such as those shown in the picture, were stretched across the streets for the night to stop the traffic. Nowadays, this role has been taken over by a road sign

when its rooms are used by the University. The arcaded courtyard is accessible at all times, so that the ancient building is always a living part of the present.

## THE BEGINNINGS OF THE COLLEGIUM MAIUS

The Collegium Maius occupies a site which at one time was part of Cracow's Jewish quarter. Historical sources and archeological reserch tell us that both houses and a synagogue stood there and that a Jewish cemetery was situated nearby. Nowadays there are hardly any traces of the former Jewish quarter which was neither large nor very populous. In the 14th century, the part of Cracow where the Collegium stands today, rose nearly 10 metres above the level of the marshy banks of the little river Rudawa. The houses were wooden, and so was the synagogue. The sloping river banks were used for the cemetery. There was then no imposing row of houses or mansions, although at the beginning of the 14th century a large house with a Gothic gable, was erected at the crossroads facing the Market Square. A gate raised a few steps above street level led to this house from the now non-existent Przecznica Street. There was also a wooden platform for the unloading of goods. Running behind the house along St. Anne's Street was a wall with a gate in it;

This was the appearance of the "lapidea magna" which the University received in 1400 for its seat. It was a two-storeyed building with a driveway, a courtyard behind and a warehouse in the back. (Drawn by Professor Wiktor Zin)

then came an outbuilding or annexe, a kind of inaccessible warehouse. The long and lofty room on the upper floor of the house was called the "palatium" after the custom of the time and was apparently particularly elegant.

This isolated house, higher than those of the Jewish newcomers, and known as the *lapidae magna*, was the property of the Pęcherz family from Rzeszotary. The deed of sale, drawn up in 1394, reads: "We Spytko, Voivode and Castellan of Cracow, hereby make it known that Mistress Małgorzata Pęcherz and her son Franciszek Pęcherz have reported to us that they have sold in its entirety to Piotr Gerardorf, burgher of Cracow, their own corner house, built of brick and situated in St. Anne's Street, together with the ground and adjoining buildings along its length and breadth, as it is separated from other houses and grounds".

Piotr Gerardorf may have been acting on the commission of King Ladislas Jagiełło or Queen Jadwiga. Within the fol-

lowing year, Gerardorf cleared the house mortgages and obligations towards the Jewish neighbours.

It was this house that was destined to play an important role: under the terms of the last will of the good Queen Jadwiga and thanks to the benevolence of Jagiełło, it became the seat of the University, and has survived — with changes, it is true — to the present day.

Whoever walks along St. Anne's Street from the Market Square, cannot fail to notice the high corner house, its gable decorated with Gothic fleurons, and its walls of rough-hewn stone. This is a part of the above-mentioned Pęcherz house and, at the same time, the oldest part of the Collegium Maius where the University took up its abode in the year 1400.

Act of restoration of the Jagiellonian University, issued by Ladislas Jagiełło on 15 July 1400. It reads in part: "We, Ladislas, King of Poland, Supreme Duke of Lithuania, see that a learned assembly adds luster and honour to Paris, how it strengthens and adorns Bologna and Padua, enlightens and exalts Prague, makes Oxford bright and fertile. Indeed we therefore acceeded to the throne and acquired the crown of the Kingdom of Poland, that we might brighten it with the brilliance of learned men, that we might by their teaching remove the shadow of deficiencies and raise her to the level of other countries..."

In the early 15th century, the influence of the Charles University in Prague upon the Jagiellonian University was considerable. The Bohemian scholars who settled in Cracow, brought with them customs and even certain architectural forms; witness thereof is the oriel-window in the façade of Collegium Maius. It is more modest than the one in Prague, has no stone flutings and sculptures but the proportions are similar and the function is the same: to provide a well-lighted place for the lector reading learned works during gatherings

## THE JAGIELLONIAN FOUNDATION

"We Ladislas, by the grace of God King of Poland, hereby make it known that we have resolved to assign for the lodgings of the masters and for the daily general gatherings of students, our house in St. Anne's Street, as measured and delimited, known as the Stefan Pęcherz House after its former owner, and later owned by Gerardorf, burgher of Cracow. This we have done so that the doctors, masters, licentiates, bachelors and students of Cracow University may freely and conveniently hold their lectures, classes and scholarly task there. We have exempted the said house from all duties, levies, taxes, neighbourly obligations, dues, court fees, legal and customary fees, and from the imposition of horse-and-cart and other charges".

This is the text of the official act by which the Pęcherz house was turned over to the University in 1400. In a further part of the same document the King granted the new foundation the right to give shelter to fugitives, a privilege usually reserved for churches, and renounced his own right of inheritance with regard to the property.

All this happened in Cracow in very much the same way as in other cities of Europe where institutions of higher learning were being established. The laws introduced in Poland were intended to conform as closely as possible to those in force in the 13th and 14th century in such famous centres of learning as Bologna, Paris, Oxford and, of course, Prague, (it should be recalled that it was mainly due to the assistance of scholars from Prague that the revival of Cracow University in

1400 was achieved so quickly and efficiently).

Let us, however, return to the new Collegium, thereafter called Maius, or *Collegium Regis Vladislai* to emphasize Jagiello's role.

The Pęcherz house was not very spacious. On the ground floor it had only few rooms, and on the upper floor a long chamber known as the "palatium" which was probably used from the beginning as the main hall for assemblies and lectures. The problem was to find lodgings for the masters and students, administrative buildings, an oratory and a room for storing the books, even if there were few of them at first. Probably not long after the move the main house was connected with the annexe, which was raised to the height of the former. Little can be deduced today from the walls themselves, since they have been reconstructed.

Documents tell us about a further extension of the Collegium at the beginning of the 15th century. An act from 1417 reads : "We Ladislas, King of Poland, seeing that due to the increase in the number of doctors and masters the house assigned for the arts college has proved too small and too confined, and is not sufficient either for the masters' lodgings or for the lectoria necessary for the lectures and classes that must be held there and wishing to supplement and enlarge the house, hereby give our royal consent and permission for Smoil to sell to the doctors and masters, i.e. to the University, two more houses which, after the decease i.e. death of the said Smoil shall belong to Us and to Our heirs".

The purchase of further land and houses, including the synagogue and the cemetery, continued throughout the whole 15th and even into the 16th century. The extension of the Collegium Maius was going on at the same time. However, it is not easy to say what the university looked like in the middle of the 15th century : it probably consisted of a group of houses next to the former Pęcherz house and connected with it in a haphazard manner and at first not even having a common courtyard. There are no relevant entries in the accounts of the time.

On the other hand, the large hall called Common Room or Stuba Communis, dating from the 15th century, has survived

The eastern façade of the Collegium, for the most part of brick, gradually came into being in the course of the 15th century, when the detached houses the University had bought from private owners were connected and reconstructed. The windows with gratings in Jagiellońska Street belong to 1st-floor rooms and to the small rooms of the University treasury. The oriel-window belongs to the Common Room and the last window of the building to the library

to the present day. "Stuba" — a word of German origin, denotes a heated room, and the adjective "communis" (common) indicates that the room was used for gatherings and as a dining hall.

15

The Common Room, with its wooden ceiling (reconstructed), wainscoted walls and Gdańsk staircase dating from the end of the 17th century (installed during the last restoration) today differs from its original appearance in the Middle Ages. Only its proportions, the arrangement of windows and, above all, the unique Gothic oriel-window have remained unchanged.

In medieval architecture the purpose of an oriel-window was to secure better and longer daylight for the interior. Let us remember that since the streets were narrow and glass not widely used, the lighting of interiors was a particularly difficult problem. Hence window-seats and oriel-windows.

From the outside, the oriel protecting into Jagiellońska Street is apsidal in shape and supported by corbels. Inside, it has a Gothic rib-vault and is lighted by five small ogival windows. The oriel was used by the lector, who during meals, read aloud serious texts (as is still done in monasteries today).

The oriel-window in the Common Room bears a strong resemblance to a similar oriel in Prague's Collegium Carolinum. It must have been built after the Prague

On the ground floor of the Collegium Maius were reading-rooms called auditoria. These were dim and not very high rooms entered through Gothic portals.

model, and this fact has a certain importance for the history of the Collegium building. As has already been mentioned, the Jagiellonian restoration of the University was largely achieved with the assistance of Czech scholars who introduced to Cracow new scientific and educational methods and University customs. This explains the construction of the oriel and its resemblance to the Prague model both in its proportions and its functions. The Cracow oriel is rather simpler and more austere in form (which, incidentally, gives it its particular aesthetic value), but its dependence on the Prague model is manifest.

In the first half of the 15th century, the Collegium Maius very clearly modelled itself on the Carolinum. The fact that the resemblance can hardly be detected today, is due to the architectural changes

The eastern façade of the Collegium Maius seen from the side of the Libraria. On the left is the gate leading to the garden. The roof of the Libraria is covered with tiles arranged in rhombs. In the background are houses in Jagiellońska Street

Situated on the 1st floor was the largest reading-room of the theologians, adorned by a Renaissance portal. Leading to professors' lodgings were various stairs and galleries added in the course of numerous reconstructions of the building

introduced later, in the second half of the century, when Bishop Zbigniew Oleśnicki discouraged contacts with Bohemia which was going through the drama of the Hussite wars.

## FURTHER EXTENSIONS

Although Jan Długosz, historian and diplomat, did not hold a chair at the University, the University had no better friend than he in the 15th century. To Długosz it owed the Law-students' dormitory in Grodzka Street, and it was Długosz who bought the grounds and houses adjoining the Collegium Maius in the south in order to facilitate the rapid expansion of the University in the 1460's.

In 1462, a dangerous fire broke out in the Dominican monastery and spread to the northern part of the city. Since most houses had shingle roofs the fire spread rapidly and consumed the part of Collegium Maius which contained the Stuba Communis. Reconstruction was started immediately and it was probably at this

time that the Common Room was covered with a ceiling and enlarged. The construction work must have lasted three years since in 1466 money was still being paid to the master-builders and masons, and the professors' meetings were "exceptionally" held outside the Common Room.

More room was still needed, however. Two years later, in the time of Rector Jan of Latoszyn, it was decided to divide the new building horizontally into three storeys, with lecture rooms on the ground floor and lodgings for twenty professors on the 1st and 2nd floor. The Latin text of the relevant decisions reads as follows: "Placuit Universitati quod in muris quos noviter edificat tria interstitia fierent, scilicet tres ordines, unus lectorium, secundus et tertius camerarum".

The building was obviously done according to one plan and took quite a long time, since in the next twenty years (1470—91) sources list numerous expenditures for the construction and furnishing of the Collegium Maius.

It was presumably at this time that the

The courtyard of the Collegio di Spagna of Bologna University is surrounded by arcades similar to those in Cracow's Collegium Maius. The arcades were used by those making their way to lectures. The courtyard was the site of festive occasions, theatre performances, etc. and was closely connected with the life of the school. In Italy, the arcades usually had arches ; in Poland, pointed Gothic arches were used. However, the two courtyards had similar proportions and, what is more important, performed similar functions

building of the Collegium Maius as a single entity planned around a large courtyard took shape. The wings were covered with uniform roofs and wooden stars led directly to the lodgings on the upper floors from the courtyard. There may also have been wooden galleries.

As a whole, the Collegium Maius was not a particularly ornate or impressive building ; in fact a functional complex of houses rather than a monumental edifice.

## ALBERTI'S THEORY

In the 14th century, in Florence and Bologna, in Milan and Rome, town-halls, palaces, cloth halls and barracks were built, with arcaded courtyards or loggias for stairs, and with heavy pillars connected by arches. In those edifices, the Gothic style, one might say, was retreating and subdued. An effect of dignity and power was achieved not so much by boldness of construction, but rather by emphasis on the weight, mass and expanse of the walls. Such is the Bargello in Florence, the Palazzo Comunale and, above all, the Collegio di Spagna in Bologna ; the latter was founded in 1364, i.e. in the same year that Casimir the Great established Cracow University which was modelled on the "studium generale of Bologna".

The architecture of the Italian trecento was for a long time not too highly appreciated because, compared to the superb and light Florentine architecture of the 15th century, with the work of Brunelleschi, Michelozzo or Alberti, it was merely a kind of prelude to the Renaissance.

At the same time, theoreticians of architecture began to have their say in Florence. All Renaissance treatises on architecture were based on the work of Vitruvius, which also served as a model to the architect Leone Battista Alberti. However, the latter's Ten Books on the Art of Building (*Libri de re aedificatoria decem*, 1450) was written from a more consistent, modern and practical point of view than that of Vitruvius.

In Chapter V of the above work, which deals with university architecture, we find the following recommendations: "The buildings to which are confined men who combine a spiritual life with the study of perfect arts, should indeed not be placed right amidst the noisy and bustling life of tradesmen, but should not be too far removed from contact with burghers — so that the scholars, as it is their duty, may become easily acquainted with human problems. And also because they form a kind of large family. In these places, people gather in great numbers to listen to lectures and to conduct disputations on spiritual matters. Hence spacious premises are needed. The buildings should be located near such public utilities as theatres, circuses, squares, where crowds gather spontaneously for pleasure and, by persuasion, warnings and religious solace may be weaned from evil and steered towards good, and from ignorance be led to the knowledge of what is best". Further on Alberti says: "The ancients, and especially the Greeks, used to put up in the centre of towns buildings called palaestras, where lovers of philosophy gathered for disputations. There were spacious rooms equipped with rows of seats, beautiful views unfolded from the many windows and a roofed colonnade surrounded a lawn. Such an arrangement would be most fitting for the kind of scholars we mentioned above. I would wish that those who have a predilection for the study of things spiritual, may always with the greatest pleasure remain in the company of true masters, in surroundings which cause no weariness or surfeit. This is why I would arrange both the grounds, the colonnade and other things like it in such a way that one could desire nothing more for one's ease. In winter gentle sunbeams would reach there, and in summertime there would be shade and a pleasant breeze..."

## HUMANISM IN THE ARCHITECTURE OF THE COLLEGIUM MAIUS

Humanism, that great intellectual movement born in Italy in the 15th century, reached Poland early. This was due to

The courtyard also served as a place of relaxation as it still does today. Members of the staff of the Jagiellonian University Museum come there to relax and for friendly chats

the numerous Polish-Italian contacts towards the end of the Middle Ages, including church relations with Rome, the political and diplomatic contacts of the Jagiellons, trade relations, and also to the Italians who had settled in Poland.

Above all, however, humanism reached Poland as a result of educational travels. Poles educated in Bologna, Padua, Rome and Naples, brought home a fund of modern knowledge and ties of friendship with Italian humanists under whose influence they remained for the rest of their lives.

Długosz, when writing his monumental history of Poland, took the work of Livius as his model. The political exile Filippo Buonaccorsi, called Callimachus settled in Poland. The most distinguished

19

young scholars from Cracow travelled to Italy to improve at the source their knowledge of ancient civilization and of Latin. They won academic degrees there, to mention only Copernicus who studied in Bologna, Padua and Ferrara or Klemens Janicki who studied in Rome. This had an unfavourable effect on the vernacular, which our 15th-century humanists neglected in favour of Latin. Latin examples were imitated and Polish was considered too common.

In the arts Italian influence is already visible in the 15th century. The tomb of Ladislas Jagiełło in Cracow Cathedral, certain mural paintings (at Niepołomice or in the Franciscan Church in Cracow), and certain craft objects bear witness to the fact that Italian influence penetrated to Poland already in the first half of the 15th century, often by way of Hungary. The process was not fully consistent: old views, and prejudices, scholastic philosophy and old laws still persisted strongly in the 15th century. It happened that people writing verses according to Virgil or Horace or investigating the world around them, would at the same time believe in astrology, alchemy or sorcery. It also happened that the same adherents of humanism would often shrink from what was considered too bold, or too light, a way of life and tried to find a more conservative way. In the history of the Jagiellonian University towards the end of the 15th century historians note a retreat in the face of the exuberance of humanism — just at the time when the Collegium Maius acquired its final architectural form.

In the field of architecture the Renaissance style came to us in the 15th century not in the lighter version of the Florentine quattrocento, but in the earlier and somewhat more conservative version of the 14th century, with its dignified and heavy buildings, courtyards surrounded by arcades, and almost fortified façades. On close analysis this style can be found in the Collegium Maius.

## THE COURTYARD AND GALLERIES

The end of the 15th and beginning of the 16th century saw a further extension of the Collegium Maius, carried out, it seems, according to plans made around 1470. From this time dates the building with a large courtyard which served as a place of recreation for students.

In July 1492, a fire broke out near the Collegium and "consumed the houses in the vicinity of St. Anne's Church together with the Collegium Maius and the newly installed clock". Reconstruction was started immediately. The Collegium Maius or "Great House" received 200 florins from the common purse of the University and 300 florins from Queen Elisabeth. Another 40 florins were added later.

Here is what we find in the records.

"In the year of Our Lord 1493, on the 1st of May, a meeting of doctors and masters as well as of professors with a regular income was convened by a message worded as follows: Excellent Doctor and Master! Come at 20:00 hours tonight to the Common Room of the Greater College of Arts in order to discuss, deliberate and pass a resolution, with the good of the University in view and by common assent, concerning the building of the same College recently destroyed by fire...

"At that meeting, after a thorough consultation of all doctors and masters of the two colleges present, in the presence and with the unanimous consent of all those having the right to vote and decide, it was resolved that the building of the Collegium Maius, unexpectedly consumed and destroyed by fire, should be rebuilt in fine style, and not only in a dignified manner and for the common use and benefit, but that it should also be restored in all details destroyed or damaged by the vehemence of fire".

Further on, the resolution states:

"The ruins shall be repaired and complemented in such a manner that in the part where the wall collapsed, a new wall shall be raised and built, beginning from the stable and reaching up to the lodging of Master Wojciech of Brudzew, i.e. as far as the College extends. It was agreed that the lodgings of doctors on the 1st floor as well as some of the auditoria should be improved and renovated to such an extent as would seem necessary for the common use and dignity".

We quote this resolution in full because it is characteristic and throws a valuable light on the matter of reconstruction. It shows what importance was attached to it and what influence the professors had on the layout of the building. We see from the resolution that the former layout of the Collegium around the courtyard was maintained, that the lectoria on the ground floor were improved and the distribution of lodgings on the upper floors retained. It was kept in mind that the building should bring "common" benefit by its fine style, by utility combined with dignity, i.e. with the appropriate artistic expression.

A recently discovered entry in the notebooks of the historian Żegota Pauli, preserved in the Jagiellonian Library, may well prove to be the most important piece of information on the history of the reconstruction of Collegium Maius:

"On 18 August 1493, the doctors concluded a contract with architect Jan concerning the construction of stairs and galleries in the Greater College up to the room with the oriel-window and that at the price of 30 florins (counting 30 groschen for one florin)".

This information is so valuable because it gives the name of the architect who undertook the building work. The newly elected Rector of the University at that time was Jan Sacranus of Oświęcim, a distinguished professor and humanist educated in Italy; it is known that in 1474 and 1475 he was a pupil of the famous humanist Filelfo in Rome.

At about the same time, another humanist died in Cracow; this was Callimachus, tutor and companion at Jagiełło's court. It may have been under his influence, too, that the courtyard of the Collegium Maius acquired the proportions and arcades so strongly reminiscent of Italian architecture. Indeed, the courtyard of the Collegium Maius, as built by architect Jan has the shape of an Italian cortile from the 14th century. The Collegio di Spagna, founded by Cardinal Egidio Albarez and still existing today, was established in Bologna in 1364. It was this building, the work of the architect Matteo Gattaponi of Gubio which became the model for the new university buildings in Cracow.

Another Italian building which the Collegium Maius also resembles strongly is the Bargello in Florence. The dependence of our Collegium on the Bargello is quite noticeable. The construction of stairs and galleries in the Bargello was commenced in 1320; the former (how much like them are the stairs in the Collegium Maius!) were built by the architect Meri di Fioravante in 1367. The Italian arcades differ in detail, of course (which should be noted), but the function, of the arcades in the Collegium Maius is the same.

The palace of the municipal guard in Florence, known as the Bargello, is a monumental edifice with an arcaded courtyard and outer staircase leading to the upper floor. This courtyard, built in the 14th century, was always greatly admired for its dignity and often imitated. In his similar structure Architect Jan in 1492 probably followed the wishes of the Cracow professors, who had in mind the stately courtyards of the Italian palaces

The Gothic vaults under the arcades of the Collegium Maius date from 1492 and are among the oldest examples of this type of vault in Poland

In Florence half of a century later, the architect Arnolfo di Cambio (1238—1310) built the palace of the Town Council — Palazzo della Signoria — also known as the Palazzo Vecchio which resembles the Bargello and also has an arcaded courtyard (built by Michelozzo in 1454 with later decorations by Vasari). The similarity between the two buildings in Florence and the Collegium Maius is obvious.

Before explaining this influence of Italian architecture, let us return for a moment to the person of Master Jan, who built the staircase and arcades in the Collegium Maius. In all probability, he can be identified with the architect Jan of Cologne who at that time became a citizen of Cracow. If, for instance we examine details of the galleries (crystal vaults, columns), we shall find certain features in common with the castle in Meissen.

This German provenance seems to belie Italian influence. And, in architectural details at many rate, Jan of Cologne who studied in southern Germany before he came to Cracow remained under the influence of South German architecture.

The plan of the whole building, on the other hand, and the Italian character of the courtyard are due to Cracow professors who were familiar with the Italian architecture of Bologna or Florence. Therefore, while one cannot go so far as to call the Collegium Maius, a Renaissance building, it is surely an expression of humanist influences in Cracow at the end of the 15th century.

Somewhat different criteria must be applied to High Gothic in Poland (from the middle of the 15th century), than in

The columns supporting the ogival arcades are carved with ornamentation reminiscent of wooden architecture

Austria, Bohemia or Germany. In Poland, High Gothic (especially in Cracow) was not an expression of the awakening of national consciousness and of the break with the universalism of the Middle Ages, as was primarily the case in Germany — but rather a turn towards the Romance south. Just as the Polish historian Jan Długosz studied Livius and referred to classical antiquity, so in the field of architecture towards the end of the 15th century, attempts were made to seek contacts with Italy which was known to be imbued with ancient culture.

At the same time, after the middle of the 15th century the influence of the German countries on the Danube was growing while cultural ties with Hungary were decreasing. After 1500, with the expansion of the trade and banking activities of the Boner family in Cracow, the influence of Nuremberg came to the fore. Certain estates, the middle class, for instance, gravitated towards Silesia and further on to Germany. While others, like the clergy, turned towards Italy. The example of the royal court, which brought Italian artists to Poland, was decisive and the magnates and gentry followed its example.

The High Gothic of the Collegium Maius cloisters, of the related Garden of Gethsemane by the Church of St. Barbara and several other Cracow monuments, reveals a knowledge of new architectural forms and of Italian art in general. And since the basis of this development is the humanism that was so strong in Cracow in the second half of the 15th century, we venture to apply to this variant of High Gothic the term humanistic. Although to interpret the shape of the courtyard as a product of Italian theories of architecture (and, in particular, of Albert's treatise on architecture) may seem rather far-fetched, there is no doubt that while it was architect Jan who designed the courtyard of the Collegium Maius the inspiration that guided him was humanism. In this "humanist" style, the architectural motifs and details remained Gothic but the layout and function were imbued by the influence of the South. This was the kind of architecture that the Cracow professors wanted.

## THE CONSTRUCTION OF THE ASSEMBLY HALL AND OF THE GABLED ROOF

The oldest surviving account books kept by the administrator or so-called Procurator of the University, dates back to the year 1507. It was started by the energetic lawyer and administrator Mikołaj of Koprzywnica, incidentally, one of the first professors to be married (by special Papal dispensation). Mikołaj's administrative role was very important, and he must be credited with the many solid as well as decorative reconstructions. He

The renovation of the Collegium Maius restored the former arrangement of roofs over the various wings. The upward thrust of the edifice is stressed by the chimneys on the roofs, the intended gables and the Gothic fleurons

The Aula Assembly Hall of the Collegium Maius has high Venetian Renaissance windows, built in 1509, probably by the Cracow architect Marek

ed, on behalf of the University, by Mikołaj of Koprzywnica.

He started by transporting the building material and then made a contract with master-builder Marek concerning the roofs. In 1507, Marek built the gabled roof over the assembly hall, crowned it with fleurons, and tiled the roofs. In the years 1507—10, the University was buying bricks and tiles from potters in the Carmelite monastery at Piasek and from the brick-kiln at Zwierzyniec. Upon the completion of the roof, Mikołaj of Koprzywnica made the following entry:

"For the weather-vane atop the gabled roof of the lectorium of the Greater College, for three cramp-irons for the said gabled roof, for big iron nails for the said gable to hold in place the stone sculptures or fleurons placed over the said gable, I paid to the hands of the said Marek three wiarduneks". (Wiardunek — medieval weight and monetary unit equivalent to 12 groschen).

The work took two years because of a shortage of funds and materials. Additional rooms were built and the sums spent on stoves, chimneys, waterspouts, galleries, latrines and cellars, increased daily. At the same time the assembly hall was furnished with a long desk under canopy painted blue and benches on oak steps. 850 Venetian glass panels were bought for the Common Room.

Let us look at the architectonic details that may be attributed to master Marek, first of all the windows of the assembly hall and at the intended gable above it.

The windows of the front façade at the corner of St. Anne's and Jagiellońska Streets date from 1507. They are divided into three parts by stone jambs.

Rising over the brick gable with shallow recesses of modest profile, are fleurons on brick supports.

The completion of the assembly hall and gabled roof in 1507 was not the last stage in the construction of the Collegium Maius. The needs of the University were increasing all the time. The 15th century brought an increase in movable property consisting above all of books but including, as we shall see, other objects as well, from scientific instruments to works of art and curios. The construction of new rooms therefore proved necessary.

who completed the building, reconstructed the library, furnished the interiors and, unlike Sacranus, preferred the Gothic architecture of Silesia.

After the construction of the italianate modern courtyard or cortile, the University appeared to be reluctant to pursue any excessive boldness of form, and did not go beyond this modest humanistic style. The conservative trend found expression in the construction of Gothic roofs over the northern wing (above the assembly hall), and of the Gothic vault of the Libraria. These works were direct-

24

The façade of the Libraria or collegiate library (1515—19) built by architect Benedykt of Sandomierz

## THE LIBRARIA

The last part of the Collegium Maius, known as the Libraria, was built during the term of office of Rector Stanisław Biel.

Actually, it is a building independent of the College itself and was treated as such for a long time. When it was put up in the years 1515—19, it was intended to serve the University as a whole.

The importance of the Libraria building in the history of Polish architecture is due not only to its form but also to the fact that we still have account books dating from the early years of the 16th century which contain detailed information on the work of construction. There are many interesting entries shedding light on medieval architectural customs in Poland and on building techniques.

Let us start with a brief description of the building.

The Libraria building abuts in the south on to the Collegium Maius and partly merges with it. The reading-room is on the upper floor and rests on cradle-vaulted rooms on the ground floor. Large rectangular windows look south. There is extensive Gothic ribbed vaulting. Between the 1st-floor gallery and the Libraria is a High Gothic sculptured portal, called

"porta aurea", which is earlier than the building itself and undoubtedly originated in the workshop of Wit Stwosz (around 1492).

The University's chief administrator, Mikołaj of Koprzywnica, whom we already know from previously mentioned accounts, made the following entry in his records:

"On Friday, the very day of St. Sigismund, 1515, I concluded a second contract with master-builder Stefan, in the presence of the following doctors and masters: Biel, Bernard, Michał of Wrocław

The Libraria is a building added to Collegium Maius on its south side. Supported by buttresses, it has large windows on the 1st floor and a roof with indented gables

and Marcin of Olkusz, concerning the building or construction of two vaults: one to be over the cellar in front of the said lodging of Doctor Bernard, the other to be made by building a wall running across the said cellar, with an arch or "boga" in about the centre of the cellar. For "propping up" the walls of the said cellar with large stones called "orczels", for building a second vault and a new wall in the small gallery of the said lodging in order to provide an entrance to the two cellars, for excavating soil to lay foundations for the above-mentioned

The Libraria is crowned by slender Gothic brick gables with pinnacles, chimneys and arches. In view of the severe Polish climate, the construction elements had to be made of stone, otherwise the architectural details in brick would have been short-lived

"neck", for installing two doors and two windows in the said cellars — the gentlemen named above being informed about all these works — for all this, I gave the above-named master-builder 6 grzywnas in all, in accordance with the said contract". ("Grzywna" — old measure of weight equal to half a pound; also, a coin with a content of about 200 grams of silver, worth 48 groschen).

Thus architect Stefan started the construction together with architect Benedykt and other Cracow master-builders, as can be seen from further accounts:

"On Tuesday, the very day of St. Margaret, when the four master-builders,

The ground-floor windows of the Libraria were covered with gratings for security. The triple window on the right has a Renaissance shape while that on the left is divided by a little Gothic Column. An escutcheon on the column bears the emblem of the architect or founder

namely Gerard, Paweł, Benedykt (from the Cracow Castle) and Stefan, came again to the Collegium to examine the new foundations of the said Library, and to consult on further work, I gave them 6 groschen for wine.

"To master-builder Stefan, for his trouble and care taken over the building and the work in the said library, since he provided the masons, journeymen and hired hands as well as the material and other necessary things, conducted the work and supervised it for the above-mentioned 21 weeks, I gave 6 grzywnas and 22 groschen".

The work was completed in 1519, when the roof was put up. As the accounts show, what we can see today — the façade in Jagiellońska Street, the ground-floor rooms, and the big L-shaped library room on the upper floor date from this period (1515—19). As usually happens numerous finishing jobs remained to be done, including the furnishing of the interior and the glazing. As late as 1523, a certain sum was remitted to pay for these jobs by Maciej Miechowita, professor of the University and famous physician.

The Libraria of the Collegium Maius was the common work of professors and architects. It was very modern and conformed to the canons of librarianship of that time, which required the reading-room to be large and the book-rests standing by the windows to have lighting from the south.

Of particular value is the information that in addition to the previous architects known to us, i.e. Jan and Marek, two more were employed, called Stefan and Benedykt.

Of the four, we know most about Benedykt but even in his case our knowledge is incomplete. Benedykt was an architect who came to Cracow from Wrocław, where he had built the southern façade of the Town Hall, no longer extant. He was a royal architect employed at the Wawel Castle and, from the middle of the 16th century, did building jobs for Sigismund I at the Wawel and in Piotrków and Sandomierz. (That is how he came to be known as Benedykt of Sandomierz.) Benedykt's work betrays distinct features of the early Renaissance style as found in Wrocław. This is true of the windows of the Libraria in the Collegium Maius, of the portals in the Wawel and architectural details which we know to have come from his atelier in Sandomierz. What we do not know is where he was educated and whether he was in any way related to the distinguished Czech architect, Benedykt Ret. Both have the same name, but we cannot tell whether this is more than just a coincidence.

As has already been mentioned, the Libraria was the last building in the Collegium Maius complex. In the history of European libraries it is one of the most valuable monuments.

## FURTHER HISTORY OF THE COLLEGIUM

The further history of the Collegium Maius up to the middle of the 17th century brought no major changes. Life followed a steady course, remote from events at Court and at the Polish Seyms, as well as from the wars which luckily spared Cracow. We do not hear of major building work in the 16th century. The University accounts record repairs of the roofs, the well, the windows and minor reconstruction work in the professors' lodgings. This shows that the building was sound and performed its function as the main seat of the University.

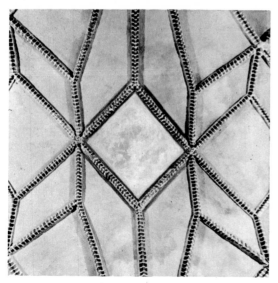

The Gothic central stellar vault in the Library (1519)

Pawilon dziedzieńca Kollegium St Jana, Kanliga w Krak...
na przeciw Bramy głowny

The Gothic wall of the courtyard as it looked around 1817. Drawing by Józef Brodowski

From the middle of the 16th century, learning in Cracow ceased to advance, not only in the fields of natural sciences and medicine, but also in philosophy and law. Theology favoured scholastic disputations and the memorization of facts prevailed everywhere.

The influx of foreign students also came to an end and after the middle of the 16th century, the buildings no longer resounded with many foreign tongues. Germany's own excellent universities were flourishing and Hungarians could no longer travel to Cracow since their country was occupied by the Turks. Foreign scholars were no longer settling in Cracow; they would only visit the city, and that less and less frequently.

At the same time, the salaries and incomes of those connected with the Collegium dropped considerably and the build-

ing was often shockingly neglected. The college was losing in importance and it is no wonder that under these circumstances, voices were raised calling for reforms. Yet at the same time, for all the shortcomings and neglect there were also bright moments bearing witness to the scholars' attachment to their university, reflected above all in bequests made by professors and other donors. At the same time, the University collections were put in order and inventoried. From 1507, a list of all gifts was kept in a special ornate book which allows us today to follow the history of some of the objects registered in it.

The Austrian occupation of Cracow in the years 1795—1809 was not a happy period in the history of the building. It was temporarily inhabited by Austrian Benedict-ines who were supposed to turn the University into a secondary school. The grand assembly hall was assigned by the authorities to serve as a granary.

## THE PSEUDO-GOTHIC

Until 1840, the Collegium Maius retained its medieval appearance intact. It is true that it ceased to perform its original role since instruction was no longer given there, nor was there a resident community of scholars. The reforms changed the structure of the University: it was now divided not into colleges but into faculties of theology, law, philosophy and medicine, for which the building proved unsuitable.

Moreover in the early 19th century little was known about architectural restoration. Along with expressions of appreciation voices could be heard — not many, it is true — demanding the demolition of the building. Fortunately for the Collegium, the University library had grown considerably and the demolition of the building would therefore have caused such great organizational difficulties that it was much easier to restore it.

In the years 1820—50, romanticism prevailed in Polish architecture, as in the rest of Europe, and the restoration of buildings in a neo-Gothic style was considered an improvement. Gothic was wrongly considered to be a product of Gothic i.e. Germanic culture and this was an additional advantage for the partitioning Powers ruling Poland, since it helped to obliterate the indigenous character of Polish towns and cities.

It is interesting to note that English Gothic was chosen which was very different from French, German or Central-European Gothic. The highly decorative English style was at that time considered to be more characteristic although when introduced into the Collegium Maius, it struck an alien note which disrupted the unity of the building.

Around 1840, Cracow came to be governed by Father Jan Schindler, an Austrian professor at the Jagiellonian University, and an exponent of Metternich's reactionary policies.

As President of the Senate of the Free City, Schindler undertook the reconstruction of the Collegium Maius in the neo-Gothic style. Under his direction, the work was accomplished by the Cracow architect, Karol Kremer. The first stage (1840—48) dealt with the eastern wing and was not successful. The façade in Jagiellońska Street was adorned by numerous embellishments, the windows were changed, and the new additions included a portal, stone tracery, rosettes beneath the moulding, and open parapets for the courtyard galleries. It was all stiff and cold, a soulless imitation of Gothic models.

The roofs suffered most of all. Kremer reduced their steep slope and replaced the tiles with zinc sheeting which was supposedly closer to the Middle Ages. On the courtyard side, he underpinned the projections of the roof with wooden corbels copied from English buildings.

The reconstruction done by Schindler and Kremer did not please everybody in Cracow. In 1848, Professor Ferdynand Kojsiewicz published an open letter accusing Kremer of mistakes and even negligence in the restoration work. But unfortunately his voice remained unheard.

Neither Schindler nor Kremer completed the reconstruction. In 1846 the former resigned as President of the Senate of the Free City and no longer took an active part in politics and the latter died in 1861, after having added a neo-Gothic

This painting from the time of the neo-Gothic reconstruction (c. 1850), was invaluable for the restoration of the original shape of the courtyard

29

Neo-Gothic details introduced in the Collegium in the 19th century were not fortunate, as can be seen in the water-colour painting by R. Alt, made in 1876

façade on the garden side. However, further reconstruction work followed their general plan until 1870. At that time, the direction was taken over by the Ministry of Education in Vienna and, for several years, it was not in Cracow but in the capital of Austria that decisions were made concerning restoration work. The Cracow architect Feliks Księżarski complied with these decisions which were to tell the truth, generally well liked and suited to an epoch that sought after rich effects.

In the years 1860—70, the northern façades (across the street from the Church of St. Anne) were demolished and flimsy Gothic ribbed vaults embellished with stucco decorations were added to the rooms (including the Jagiellonian assembly hall).

The Collegium Maius, thus altered in appearance, was turned over to the Jagiellonian Library which remained there until World War II. It was now a huge collection, no longer on a University but on a national scale, and the rooms of the Collegium Maius, at one time intended for about one hundred thousand volumes, could not hold nearly a million. Additional shelves and bookcases were placed

wherever possible and the ceilings were propped up with beams.

In the years 1934—39, a new library building was erected.

In 1940, already under Nazi occupation, the books were moved to the new building. The Collegium Maius was deserted and was taken over by a historical institute devoted to the work of Germanization.

## RESTORATION IN THE 20TH CENTURY

It was with some trepidation that the restoration of the Collegium Maius was considered after the Second World War. The building was in a very bad condition. Many years of neglect and the Nazi occupation had taken a heavy toll and local carelessness went so far that in 1945 a poultry exhibition and an old school furniture store were installed on the 1st floor.

The idea of restoring the buildings' original appearance had been mooted in University circles for years. In the second half of the 19th century the art collec-

30

tions of the University had grown considerably, largely due to the efforts of Józef Łepkowski. Various donors (Konstanty Przeździecki, Edward Rastawiecki, Władysław Czartoryski) had offered valuable collections which, although plundered by Nazi dignitaries, required adequate room after World War II. The Collegium Maius seemed admirably suited for that purpose.

The work undertaken in the years 1949—64 was guided by the principle that the Collegium Maius should be restored as faithfully as possible to its appearance prior to the 19th-century renovations. It was decided to eliminate pseudo-Gothic elements wherever possible; not only the external embellishments of the façades but also the partitions of floors and interiors. The large rooms, with pseudo-Gothic vaults, had been created at one time (in the years 1840—70) because

Entrance to the garden from Jagiellońska Street. The gate built in 1964 is modelled on Cracow's baroque gates

This Renaissance portal with the emblems of Poland, Lithuania, Sigismund I and Queen Bona, was assembled in 1960. The emblems were found in various parts of the Collegium. The doorframe is from the former Poorhouse in Wiślna Street

the Library needed storage space. Since the Jagiellonian Library had moved to its new building in 1940, there was no point in preserving these store-rooms which, moreover, were of a most unpractical shape. Detailed plans, views and photographs of the old Collegium Maius were in existence and entire parts of walls as well as various fragments of the old building had survived. There was no justification in preserving the alien pseudo-Gothic character which was eminently unpractical although obviously, the building's original appearance could not be restored everywhere. The façade on the garden side had been rebuilt so thoroughly that it was hardly possible to change it now.

Consultations, and historical and architectural research lasted through the whole of 1949. At the same time, the University Museum began to revive and took over room after room in the building. Precious relics of the past, mementos, portraits, old scientific instruments were

The baroque portal (c. 1620) has been reconstructed strictly according to preserved data. For reasons of conservation, only replicas of the 15th-century emblems have been placed above the gate

gathered in the Collegium while offices and stores were being moved out. Car accessories stores, the Voivodship Archives, school furniture stores and, finally the University's own building department as well as other incidental lodgers, had to find new homes. By January 1950, in the first year of Poland's six-year economic plan, the eastern wing and half of the northern wing were cleared and the work of restoration could proceed.

To begin with, Bergmann's neo-Gothic vault from 1870 was removed from the Jagiellonian assembly hall, then the ceilings and vaults along St. Anne's Street disappeared and the pseudo-Gothic windows embellished with stucco decorations were removed from the Jagiellońska Street façade. Every day uncovered unknown centuries-old details, such as portals, windows, remnants of frescoes. Every day brought to light new, sometimes very valuable, discoveries and conservation

plans had consequently to be modified. Even the original layout of rooms and floors was uncovered.

The first years of reconstruction were the hardest. In the spring of 1950, the Collegium Maius disappeared behind scaffolding, the roofs on the eastern side were removed, the interiors were ripped up from cellars to attics. And this was only the beginning.

By this time, new principles and methods of conservation were already in force all over Europe. In earlier days, in the Victorian period, and especially towards the end of the 19th century, the restoration of monuments was conceived solely as the strict conservation of extant architectural fragments and no one entertained the possibility of reconstructing earlier elements or removing later accretions. This positivism in conservation principles was abandoned after World War II when entire buildings or indeed towns were reconstructed from ruins because one could not allow their disappearance. The renovation of the Collegium Maius undertaken at that time, therefore aimed not only at reconstruction, but also at restoring to the interior of the building its former function of university college. It was recognized that a building of this type acquires in the course of years works of art, furniture and various related objects and that this very process of accretion creates a certain valid picture of the past.

In the years 1950—56 the Collegium Maius was reconstructed and furnished. With the financial help of the Ministry of Higher Education and the Praesidium of the Council of Ministers, the ceilings and roofs were restored to their former Gothic appearance. The foundations were reinforced and a new drainage system was installed. After the Jagiellonian Hall, Common Room and Libraria were completed in 1955 and opened as a museum work began on the courtyard staircase and arcades. There it was necessary to restore the former function of the staircase as a communication route leading directly from the courtyard, as in the Bargello Palace in Florence. The entire restoration of the Collegium was supervised by Professor Alfred Majewski from the Faculty of Architecture.

*Collegium Maius*   *Customs*

# BACKGROUND

The Jagiellonian University had to function under difficult circumstances. It is true that until the end of the 15th century its development did not differ from that of other similar universities elsewhere; the high point of this development was probably when its professors of law were invited to participate in the Ecumenical Councils. In the second half of the 15th century, mathematics and astronomy flourished in Cracow. But from the beginning of the 16th century, the University was involved in social and religious conflicts which it was unable to understand, let alone to counter. Cracow was far removed from the great centres of science in the West and as royal patronage lessened in the 17th century the indifference of the public towards the University also increased. As chancellors the bishops of Cracow were despotic and frequently considered asceticism or bigotry to be the sole means of education; their attitude to secular learning was hostile. At the same time, the professors often embraced a comfortable quietism which militated against scientific progress. On the other hand, the University was more than once saved from a sorry plight by the high moral standards of the professors, their democratism and ties with the broad masses of people through secondary schools scattered all over Poland. In the period of the Swedish "deluge", the University was first in Poland, even before Częstochowa, to assume a proper attitude towards the invaders, which strengthened its position in the public opinion.

Financially, the University was supported by the generosity of individuals, above all by its professors and alumni. In the 18th century, when reforms became necessary, Hugo Kołłątaj coped very well with this difficult task. In 1809, as the Austrians were just about to close down the University, the army of Prince Józef Poniatowski liberated Cracow. Then came the time of the Free City of Cracow, by no means an easy period but at least one of home rule. Later on, when Austrianization threatened again, Galicia obtained autonomy and a considerable degree of freedom of action (1860—70). Amidst all these changes and ordeals, there were always men dedicated to the interests of their institution.

The collections of Collegium Maius thus reflect the long history of the University and of Polish culture. In many instances, the small and inconspicuous objects preserved here tell us much about the past, about people and events.

This applied not only to historical facts but also to legends concerning the Collegium. These are not of course, corroborated in documents but their echoes are now and then unexpectedly discovered within the College walls. In the 15th century, bricked-up arcades were uncovered six times, and the seventh time, a treasure-trove was found in the garden in 1956. Until recently, hardly anyone believed the legends about witchcraft which circulated persistently in Cracow, but traces of such practices have been discovered concealed in vaults or etched on brick walls.

Here is what Jan Śniadecki wrote in 1802 about the University and therefore also about our Collegium:

"It was an ancient structure from the Middle Ages, with laws, internal government and ceremonial quite similar to those that can still be found today in the two English Universities, Oxford and Cambridge. When visiting these English academies in 1787, I had the impression that I was seeing the old customs and ceremonials of the Cracow academy. The three faculties of philosophy, theology and law were housed in three colleges: in the Minor or so-called Artistarum Collegium lived philosophers and mathematicians. The Major or Jagiellonian College housed the senior or "royal" professors of philosophy and mathematics as well as doctors and professors of theology. The Juridical College was only for doctors and professors of law. Each member was known as minor or juridical colleague after the College to which he belonged. Only they could attend the general University sessions and had the right to vote. The sessions were also attended by doctors of medicine, admitted to the University and living in the city; as in the two academies named above, there were no medical studies in Cracow."

## UNIVERSITAS

When translating the Latin "universitas" into Polish in the 18th century as "wszechnica" (university), the Cracow professor and director of the Jagiellonian Library, Jacek Przybylski, did not properly grasp the medieval meaning of the term. He believed that "universitas" denoted a place where all disciplines were taught according to a uniform system. In fact it was a term used to describe the universality or in other words the corporation or community of teachers and students, and the rights and privileges granted to them. King Stephen Batory came closer to this concept of a University when he stated in 1578: "Among the parts of our Commonwealth, the Cracow Academy is both useful and necessary". So it was indeed, at least in the opinion of the professors: Universitas Cracoviensis was in fact an independent and separate corporation, her status being in principle equal to that of the gentry. This is the background against which the

history of the University unfolds — a history which many consider to have been praiseworthy only in the Middle Ages. This is the background too against which were shaped its laws, organization, educational and civic role, customs, opinions, disputes and traditions; not to mention the mistakes and examples of obscurantism from which the history of the Jagiellonian University has not been free. Yet this independence enjoyed by professors, students, and their very buildings, this freedom of instruction and jurisdiction, attracted many people. "Do not think, Gentlemen, that this paltry sum of ten grzywnas is what makes us stay with the Academy, — said Krzysztof Najmanowicz to the gentry majority in the Seym in 1633 — it is the dignity of this place that attracts people to us, and *libertates and immunitates* keep them here in poverty and modesty".

It was this very *libertates et immunitates* on which the *universitas* was based. In 1535, Sigismund I raised professors to the ranks of the nobility and though the privilege did not become effective in practice and did not properly protect the teaching profession against arbitrary government, yet something of its spirit radiated into the 17th and 18th century and remained noticeable up to the time of the Kołłątaj reform.

The same forces that drove the University to stress its independence in relation to ecclesiastical and secular rulers also stimulated fear of change and of new currents in science. Scientific stagnation was accompanied by a decline in character and moral, by excessive leniency towards the students, by attempts to make an easy living through the composition of panegyrics or almanachs. There were bright moments, too, like the determined opposition to the Swedish invaders in 1655, which surely was the source of inspiration for Prior Kordecki's defence of Częstochowa, the support given to provincial schools, and the great generosity with which professors supported dormitories for poorer students. The University also when necessary gave its support in affairs of state: Casimir Jagiellon borrowed 2 thousand ducats for the war against the Teutonic Knights, Sigismund I borrowed 400 ducats and Ladislas IV also borrowed money from the University. To

The Jagiellonian stone eagle, carrying the letter "S" in honour of Sigismund I, most certainly came from the workshop of Italian stonecutters employed at the Wawel Castle

Many people believe that in the 15th century the University was primarily a school, actually, it was a kind of scientific institute called upon not only to educate youth, but to serve the State. The role played by our University in the Middle Ages could be compared to that of a scientific academy or a committee for scientific affairs, with law, astronomy and mathematics — as well as theology and philosophy, of course — being the most important disciplines.

On this aspect of university affairs there is much interesting material in the Jagiellonian library, including the 15th-century manuscript codices relating to the Councils of Constance and Basel. Cracow professors not only took part in them as legal and diplomatic advisers to the Polish kings but also assiduously collected historical material, Council notes and opinions, especially since the Jagiellonian University, like the Sorbonne, favoured the superiority of Council over Pope. In the 19th century, some, otherwise very distinguished Polish historians (e.g. Władysław Wisłocki) made light of this work (in particular that of St. John of Kęty) which they dismissed as nothing more than the copying of Council records, a task unworthy of scholars. In fact, the material relating to the history of international law and to the political and social thought of the 15th century in the possession of the Jagiellonian Library is of immense value. This also is true of the natural sciences. Astronomical treatises, manuscripts with miniatures, scientific cyclopaedias, constitute an inexhaustible source for the history of world science, and is certainly too little known outside Poland and, which is worse, not always properly appreciated by Polish scientists. In the 15th century Cracow University became convinced of the importance of close political and cultural ties between Poland and the Roman-Catholic Church although it should be emphasized that this did not imply complete submission to the interests of the Church. In the 16th and 17th century for instance, the University carried on a long struggle against the Jesuit order which was not so much about doctrine as about the independence of Polish thought and culture from non-Polish interests and aspirations.

help the Kościuszko insurrection, the University offered its entire treasury, accumulated through many centuries, and added to it valuable surveying instruments. Students fought in the defence of Cracow in 1587, in 1655 and in 1794, not to mention the liberation struggles in the 19th and 20th centuries.

Among the professors, some were of noble character and others poor in spirit, with human qualities and faults, as in any walk of life. They formed a body of learned men mainly of peasant and middle class in origin. "Do not bow to me, a simple man, but to the velvet I am wearing", Marcin of Wadowice once said as he walked down the street in the Rector's gown and people greeted him respectfully. On the whole, professors led a modest, semi-cloistered life and enjoyed public esteem as the "Cracow academicians".

The portrait of Ladislas Jagiełło by Leopold Loeffler, made in 1864, was based on the King's tomb effigy

## WHY "JAGIELLONIAN"?

A few years after the revival of the University, it became clear how greatly it was needed as an ally and not only as the leading royal school, by the King, the State, the clergy and the nobility in the struggle they waged on the international scene against the Teutonic Knights. The recently discovered letters of the eminent jurist Paweł Włodkowic, professor and Rector of the University, provide new evidence that it was at the University that diplomatic arguments for the King were elaborated. From the Council of Constance, Włodkowic wrote in 1415: "Your Majesty will receive more detailed, clear and complete information from the doctors and masters of the University in Cracow when they acquaint themselves with the reports and annexes sent by me. Your Royal Majesty thinks fit to bestow particular care and generous royal favours upon this University, to the great advantage and honour of Your Kingdom". Thus wrote Włodkowic to the King, stressing that the University was a State institution, and at the same time recalling to the king his duty of taking care of the University. As a matter of fact, one could hardly reproach the King with lack of good will. He was a man of keen intelligence and judgement, which he demonstrated on the battlefield of Grunwald in 1410, in his dealings with the Papal State, with Sigismund of Luxemburg, with Witold and also in his revival of the University and the support he gave it. Although he was probably guided in this by the nobles of Little Poland, yet in the final count the credit and glory for it go to Jagiełło.                           •

The generous attitude towards the University shown by Jagiełło, by his sister Alexandra (who offered a gold chain preserved to this day), by his son Casimir and by his grandsons (Frederic, John Albert, Sigismund I), bring us to the next problem around which many misunderstandings have accumulated, namely to the J a g i e l l o n i a n University.

Objections are often raised that the name is new, was officially introduced in the Statutes of the University only in the period of the Free City of Cracow (in 1818 or even later) and that it is inaccurate because the founder was not Jagiełło but Casimir the Great. One hears or reads — even in works by distinguished historians — that the adjective Jagiellonian is unjustified since in the Middle Ages it was first called *Studium Generale Universitatis Cracoviensis* (in the 15th century), then *Academia Cracoviensis* or even *Gymna-*

sium (in the 16th century), later *Universitas, Alma Mater* and Main Crown School (the latter from the times of Kołłątaj), University or "Wszechnica" (the term invented by Przybylski), and then the University of Cracow or again the Academy. Yet, since the 15th century, the University has always emphasized its renewal or "Re-foundation" by Jagiełło. Other medieval universities, also made use of the name of the founding monarch (e.g. in Prague, Vienna, Leipzig, etc.) thus emphasizing their dependence on the State authority. Time and again (e.g. in the year 1423) we read about the "Collegium serenissimi regis Wladislai Regis Poloniae" or the College of King Ladislas as

the main seat of the University, the Collegium Maius, was called.

On the 15th-century seal used by the praepostor Collegium Maius is called the College of King Ladislas, and the arms of Lithuania together with the Hungarian cross of Jadwiga, serve to stress the role

This painting, done about 1620 by Tomaso Dolabella, a Venetian artist settled in Cracow, represents Ladislas Jagiełło and Jadwiga kneeling at the foot of the Cross. They are accompanied by saints, among whom is Professor Jan of Kęty patron of the University

This portrait of Queen Jadwiga by Antoni Piotrowski (1900), is an imaginary likeness of the queen whose memory lives on in the University even today

played by Jagiełło and Jadwiga in the revival of the University. Another illustration of this is the votive painting from the beginning of the 16th century which Sigismund I had hung at Jagiełło's grave around 1520, and which we know from a copy. In the centre of the painting is the University building held up by Jagiełło and Jadwiga.

The University has always showed its gratitude to the memory of Jagiełło and of his family. In the 15th century,

Preserved in the University collections is this woodcut block representing Ladislas Jagiełło on the throne, surrounded by State emblems. It was made around 1580, and based on the king's seal

The coat of arms of the patron of the University, Frederick Cardinal Jagiellon, with an eagle on the escutcheon, a hat and mitre, comes from the atelier of Wit Stwosz and was executed in 1493

Professor Jan of Kluczbork delivered a speech in honour of Jagiełło, in 1513 a requiem mass was celebrated for any Jagiellons who died abroad, and later Latin odes were composed in honour of the family. Whenever they appeared at the University, kings and queens belonging to the Jagiełło dynasty were given a particularly warm welcome, one of the reasons why the University felt compelled to support the candidature of Batory to the Polish throne was the fact that he was married to a Jagiellon princess.

From the beginning of the 17th century, the Jagiellonian traditions in the University grew even stronger. Outward evidence of this was the large painting of the founders — Jadwiga and Jagiełło — by Tomaso Dolabella hung in the assembly hall. The University at that time commenced its struggle for independence from the Jesuit order, in the course of which it readily referred to its glorious past in the Jagiellonian era in order to emphasize its traditions. In those days there were constant references to the Jagiellonians ; the University had a handsome copy made of the foundation act and commissioned S. Bianchi to paint the portraits of Jadwiga and Jagiełło.

The University must have attached great importance to these portraits, since a little later, around 1660, large and very imposing portraits were also ordered for the assembly hall, to be painted by Jan Trycjusz. The merits of Casimir the Great were not forgotten in the 17th century but the Jagiellons were all the more remembered.

In the year 1662, Marcin Radzymiński, professor and historian of the University, donated a marble plaque (called *Ara gratiarum* — Altar of gratitude) with a panegyrical inscription in honour of the founders of the University — Casimir the Great and Jadwiga and Jagiełło. At the time of the University's struggle with the despotic bishops of Cracow — Piotr Gembicki and Andrzej Trzebicki — it was Radzymiński's intention to show that the University held itself to be dependent solely on Polish kings, successors of Jagiełło. It is true that the University at this time had to pay for this love of independence by a lowering of its standards but on the other hand, it should be stressed that the Jagiellonian traditions helped the University more than once.

In the 18th century, when the need for reforms was strongly felt but faced with reluctance the University again invoked the Jagiellonian traditions in its appeals to the Seyms, the bishops and the king, for aid and protection. In the year 1764, in his speech addressed to Stanislas Augustus Rector Biegaczewicz recalled that

"this is the Jagiellonian Academy, and thereby yours, Your Majesty".

Casimir the Great's role was commemorated by the publication of the foundation act of 1364 after 1780 and Bacciarelli's painting of the foundation of the Univer-

In 1820, Rector Sebastian Sierakowski conceived the idea of decorating the assembly hall of the Collegium Maius with paintings representing the history of the University. He entrusted the task to Michał Stachowicz. Here is the scene of the restoration of the University by Ladislas Jagiełło

The marble coat of arms of Queen Jadwiga and, at the same time, of the Kingdom of Hungary, is carved on the well in Collegium Maius

sity by Casimir for Warsaw's Royal Castle (the work is known to us today only from sketches and copies); however, Jadwiga, Jagiełło and the Jagiellons, somehow retained a greater place in the Cracovians' affection.

From the middle of the century, the term Jagiellonian appeared ever more frequently. Gradually, the Collegium Maius came to be known as the "Jagiellonian House". The Primate Michał Poniatowski when writing of his intention to expand the premises of the University library in 1787, used the words "In collegio Jagellonico".

In the Age of Enlightenment, the name of Jagiełło was in constant use and is found both in panegyric prints (the earliest being Kosicki's *Manipulus Jagellonicae Palladis,* 1726), and in the polemics of Cracow professors with their adversaries (*Retort of the Cracow Academicians,* 1774) :

*"You are poking fun at devils, at monks*
*and at Cracow,*
*And yet this is the mother and the*
*fountain head of all learning,*
*The Academy, founded by Jagiełło,*
*For centuries the cradle of so many*
*great men ...*

In 1788, J. A. Putanowicz stressed in his *Pictures of Polish Kings and Princes*: "It was Jagiełło who adorned Cracow with the Academy", at that time, the name Jagiellonian College was universally adopted for the Collegium Maius and the assembly hall became known as the "Jagiellonian Room".

On the marble plaque over the portal leading to the hall appears an inscription composed in elaborate Latin by Jacek Przybylski and commemorating the visit paid by Stanislas Augustus in 1787. The University accounts from that time note : "Expenditure has been voted for the marble with an inscription over the door of the Jagiellonian Room, on the occasion of His Majesty's visit".

We also find the following entry : "4 zlotys paid to masons for taking down the chimneys in Collegio Jagellonico".

The closer the end of the century and the end of the old Republic approached, the more often the term Jagiellonian appears in sources. The greater the difficulties which confronted the professors, the more willingly they looked back upon the glorious past, as indeed did the city and the entire country, especially in the dreary years of Austrian occupation in Cracow (1795—1809).

In 1810, Józef Sołtykowicz delivered before Frederick Augustus, Duke of Warsaw, a eulogy of the University, in which he made several references to the Jagiellons. To commemorate this visit a plaque was placed in the Nowodworski College with an inscription stating that the Duke visited "Regiam Casimiri Magni et Jagellonum institutionem, almam studiorum universitatem" (the royal institution of Casimir the Great and of the Jagiellons, the university — nourisher of students). In a memorandum of 1814 on the situation of the University, we find the following eloquent statement : "The age of the Jagiellons was happiest for the Academy and for the sciences".

In Cracow the Collegium Maius was always referred to as the "Jagiellonian building" or "Jagiellonian house". The growing library at this time also received the name "Jagiellonian".

At that time, Rector Sebastian Sierakowski commissioned the Cracow artist Michał Stachowicz to decorate the assembly hall, now universally known as the Jagiellonian Room. No wonder therefore that Jerzy Samuel Bandtkie, in his "History of the Library of the Jagiellonian University" in 1821, wrote at the beginning of his work : "In the year 1400, Ladislas Jagiełło founded anew the Cracow University, to this day called Universitas Studiorum Cracoviensis Jagellonica".

In the year 1817, the official name "Jagiellonian University" was introduced into the statutes of the University : "The ancient Cracow Academy, founded by the generosity of Jagiellonian kings, shall retain the name of Jagiellonian University to crown the memory of its benefactors". After 1831, this title began to annoy the "tutelar courts" of the Free City. When the new statutes were published the title of Jagiellonian University was omitted. However, it was used all the more eagerly and only then won wide popularity. When at a later date (1875), it was proposed to adopt for the sake of historical accuracy, the name of Casimir-and-Jagiellonian University, the Academic Senate, after hearing the relevant arguments, deferred the decision on the change of name to further consideration. As can be seen, the name was formed by several hundred years of history and is a result both of traditions and views prevailing in Cracow and of the University's struggle for its independence from the partitioning Powers.

in the rim (*Sigillum Universitatis Studii Cracoviensis Generalis Sanctus Stanislaus Vladislaus R. Polon.*). It is difficult to say to what extent the seal was connected with the University and to what

The two maces placed above the entrance to the Collegium Maius are the University's oldest coat of arms and date from the end of the 15th century. In the 16th century, a crown was added to the maces to symbolize the University's dependence on the State. Apart from the crossed maces, the University also used on its seals the emblem of the Polish eagle held by St. Stanislas. In the 17th and 18th centuries, the escutcheons were richly ornamented

## THE COAT OF ARMS

The arms of the Jagiellonian University are two crossed gold maces placed on a blue escutcheon with a crown overhead (above the maces or above the escutcheon). The crown indicates that this is a royal or State University, and not episcopal, city or provincial, that it is to say independent of local authorities.

The oldest University seal dates from the times of Jagiełło (1420). It was revived in 1887 and it is now used on doctor's diplomas. It represents entirely different arms, namely the figure of St. Stanislas and, in front of him, an escutcheon with the Polish eagle and a double inscription

extent with the person of the royal founder and patron. The latter is more likely.

The origin of two crossed maces as the University arms is not clear. When did this emblem come into use ? The oldest known specimen is the escutcheon cut in stone in the Collegium Maius, dating from the second half of the 15th century (around 1470). Here there is no crown above the arms.

Professor Jan Brożek mentions in "Gratis" (1625) that "in the reign of Jagiełło, there were long deliberations as to what arms might be given to the Academy: after various councils, it was decided that, as the noble Chapter of Cracow has three crowns (in a blue field), so the

Maces are everywhere used by Universities as a symbol of independence won in the Middle Ages. The Cracow maces are among the world's oldest, especially the mace offered by Queen Jadwiga which probably dates from the end of the 14th century, although this has not retained its original form. The second mace, a gift of Zbigniew Cardinal Oleśnicki, dates from the middle of the 15th century. The third, bequeathed by Frederic Cardinal Jagiellon, is from the beginning of the 16th century

Academy should have two sceptres, and this is confirmed by other authors, too". Antoni Karbowiak, historian of education, states (1887) that when the old seals from the 15th century were lost during the Swedish wars, new seals were ordered (1659). To the two maces, a crown was added so as to distinguish the new seal from the old ones. This may have been the case with the seal, but the emblem of crossed maces with a crown is known to us from earlier times. It can generally be said that in contravention of the principles of heraldry the arms of the Jagiellonian University in the past made use of various emblems and symbols, depending on the time and the prevailing style. In the main, however, the crossed maces with a crown above them won approval and were used in many different combinations in the 18th and 19th centuries. Crossed insignia are a familiar form in heraldry. Suffice it to recall the keys of St. Peter, as the symbol of Papal power, or crossed swords, the arms of the Saxon dynasty of the Wettins. A mace and

sword crossed is frequently the emblem of lord-mayors in England, while in Italy crossed maces are found on chemist's jars. Finally, two crossed maces, like those in Cracow, are also used by the University of Tübingen, founded in 1477. The Tübingen arms have appeared since the 16th century. The colours (gold and blue) are the same, and who knows whether it was not from Cracow that the University of Tübingen borrowed its arms?

The faculties also had their separate coats of arms. Not all of them have survived to our day. St. Jadwiga of Silesia, the patron-saint of Queen Jadwiga, seems to have appeared on the coat of arms of the faculty of arts. The Collegium Maius had its own seal with arms and inscription (the Holy Virgin and Jagiełło's "Pursuit"). In the 18th century, the arms of the University undergo various changes but in general the two crossed maces appear at all times until our own day. Generally accepted as the motto of the University is the Latin phrase: *Plus ration quam vis* (Reason above force).

# INSIGNIA

Universities (among other institutions) use sceptres or maces as insignia of authority. Rectors and deans also wear chains, rings, medals and other decorations or insignia of authority (e.g. seals) which are handed over to them with due ceremony by their predecessors. In principle, the rector does not hold the mace himself; it is carried before him or placed in front of him on his desk.

The Jagiellonian University has in its possession maces from various epochs, as well as many other insignia and jewels that make up the University treasury.

There are at present fourteen maces: three from the 15th century (donated by Queen Jadwiga, Cardinal Oleśnicki and Frederick Cardinal Jagiellon), one from the 16th century (Cardinal Maciejowski), six from the 19th and 20th centuries (now used by the deans), one Jubilee mace from 1900 (from Vilna), two gilded ivory maces from the 19th century (donated by the Przeździecki family). The fourteenth mace — of the Faculty of Pharmacy — was given to the Medical Academy in Cracow upon its establishment in 1949.

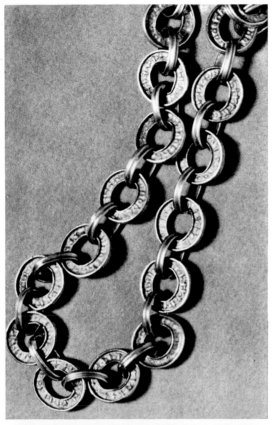

Among the Rector's treasures is the gold chain donated by Alexandra of Mazovia, sister of Jagiełło. It most probably dates from the 6th century. The motif of joined beaks is repeated on the links of the chain

Chains are more numerous. The gold chain of 128 links was a gift of Princess Alexandra of Mazovia, Jagiełło's sister. Other chains date from the 19th and 20th centuries. Five among them were acquired in 1862, before the University's five hundredth anniversary and the sixth — the rector's grand chain — in 1900. In connection with the increased number of pró-rectors and the six hundredth anniversary in 1964, six more chains were procured.

There also is a large number of rings. One of them — the Rector's grand ring (donated in 1900 by the Province of Great Poland) is still used by the Rector. The oldest one is a 15th-century gold ring (a gift of Castellan Rudawski) with the Rector's arms engraved on it in the 17th century. Then come rings received from various donors in the 19th and 20th centuries.

The earliest seals from the 15th—18th centuries are missing, but there are several newer ones including: two Rector's seals (large and small) and a seal stamp used on diplomas. Engraved on these seals are the oldest arms of the University: the eagle on a shield held by St. Stanislas. The old seals were lost during the Swedish invasion and in the fire of the Collegium Iuridicum in 1714.

survived to the present day, namely : the Collegium Maius, the Collegium Minus at the corner of Gołębia and Jagiellońska Streets, and the Collegium Iuridicum at No. 53 Grodzka Street. The medical college could probably be located at its original address, i.e. No. 51 Grodzka Street but its academic traditions were discontinued long ago.

In the 18th century, there was also the institution known today as the Kołłątaj College, which at one time belonged to the faculty of natural sciences, and the astronomical observatory in the botanical gardens. To this list we must add the dormitories or students' hostels where certain lectures or classes were also held, the Nowodworski secondary school, and the university Church of St. Anne.

Colleges had a number of small rooms, lectoria and household quarters, and one larger room called Stuba Communis, used for meetings and for midday and evening meals. In the Collegium Maius the ground floor was occupied by the lectoria (only one, the theologians' lectorium, was on the upper floor), while the rest of the building was occupied by professors' lodgings (19 of them in all) and by domestic quarters.

The colleges depended on their own incomes which consisted of a true jungle

Two of the many University rings : the golden ring from the late 15th century (with the crest engraved later) and the Rector's grand ring with a sapphire, donated by the province of Great Poland in 1900

## THE ORGANIZATIONAL STRUCTURE

In accordance with 15th c. University laws and customs, which prevailed in Cracow for four hundred years, the buildings of the various colleges were attached to the faculties of theology, philosophy, law and medicine. The medical college soon disappeared but three colleges have

of bequests, grants, investments and interest in which even the best specialists in the history of the University can hardly find their way about. Kołłątaj tried to tidy them up, but as this was already after the first partition of Poland he could not do much. In the 19th century, the grants and investments were lost altogether.

A resolution from 1449 recommended that "those selected as members of the Collegium Maius should be men of talent and merit, expert in learning, and of well-tested morals". Regard should mainly be given to merit. And, indeed, throughout the history of the University we come across people, mostly of middle class or peasant origin, who attained high academic status through hard work alone. This was a phenomenon of national importance in view of the gentry's privileged position.

The head of the University was the Rector (with juridical powers); he represented the University outside, presided over the Council and, as a rule, did not interfere in the administration of the colleges. Until the Kołłątaj reform there was one administrative organ for the University as a whole, another for the colleges and dormitories. If we add to this the role of the Chancellors of the University — since Jagiełło's day, this post was held ex officio by the bishops of Cracow — we realize how complex the system of administration was. The post of Chancellor was abolished by Kołłątaj, acting on behalf of the National Education Commission.

From the old "conclusions" or resolutions, we can learn a great many facts about University life, and especially the Collegium Maius. Meetings were attended by senior professors — "omnes doctores, decanos, licentiatios, magistros promotos et collegiatos utriusque Collegii at alias de facultate artium" — but this was in principle rather than in actual practice. In due course a special council or Senate evolved.

Meetings were convened by special written announcements, and members were expected to appear at the indicated time, in academic dress, and wearing their insignia. After an introductory prayer the Rector presented the matter to be discussed and members spoke in order of seniority.

The Rector, Pro-rector and Deans use chains a hundred years old, dating from the University's 500th anniversary celebrations (1864)

The maces now used by the University, with figures of famous men: Casimir the Great adorns the Rector's mace, Sebastian Petrycy that of the former Medical Faculty and the naturalist Emil Godlewski the elder that of the Department of Biology and Geology

At the head of the Collegium Maius was an elected senior, called the Praepostor, who looked after the building and the adjacent garden. It was also his duty to make sure of orderly behaviour and quiet, not only within the Collegium, but also outside. When a goldsmith established his workshop in the "foundry" courtyard, between the Collegium Maius and the Nowodworski College, the members of the Collegium campaigned against the noisy intruder and eventually managed to purchase the courtyard in 1510.

This is how Professor Józef Putanowicz describes some laws and customs of the Collegium Maius in his book *On the Internal and External State of the Academy* (in 1774):

"The College has its half-yearly administrator with two councillors; who are responsible for the office of internal policy on the statutes of the assembly, and the care of the table. It is his duty to convene the meetings of doctors and professors as need arises, to record the results of meetings, to collect rents and manage them according to the founders' will, to give orders to the domestic staff, to inform the *Procurator Universitatis* in advance about all necessary repairs, to submit annual reports on dates fixed, to make sure the College is closed and guarded so that professors or their servants may not amuse themselves in town until late or spend the night outside College, and to punish in accordance with the statutes those guilty of this offense". "(...) The collegiates have a common table, which is quite meagre and ordinary, and in view of their meagre incomes, content themselves with dinner only. Their servants, according to the statutes and cus-

48

toms of the College, should attend school while serving their masters; on certain days they receive midday and evening meals from the funds of the assembly (...)" The administration and financial status of the University was also described by Jan Śniadecki:

"Each particular college administered its own revenues and incomes. The Procurator of the University was the treasurer responsible for collecting if necessary by legal action, the incomes of the University as a whole, of the faculties, and of the charities for the poor. He paid the income collected to the faculties, which divided them among their members, to professors of those chairs which had their separate funds, and assigned the students' incomes to the administrators of scholarships. The general income was divided equally among all members; only the Rector and the Procurator, who had no separate pay for their function, received a double share. There was a reserve fund called the "caecus" in which one person's share was always deposited for emergencies. The philosophical faculty, while the most numerous, was the poorest of all. It had an annual income of a few thousand Polish zlotys; this money was divided unevenly, among teaching members of the faculty on St. Margaret's day in July, and these stipends were therefore known as Margaritales. An external professor received from 8 to 40 zlotys, depending on the importance of his lessons and on the number of pupils he could produce. The members of the College and Cracow professors received from 40 to one hundred zlotys".

The University treasury contained a valuable collection of jewelry donated at various times from the very beginning, i.e. from the revival of the University by Jagiełło in 1400. Other gifts bestowed by kings and noble patrons included above all insignia, but also tapestries and silverware. The treasury survived intact until 1794, when the University offered all these valuables for the financing of the Kościuszko insurrection and not for the canonization of St. John of Kęty as Kołłątaj erroneously maintained. The latter was financed by the sale of jewelry offered at the Saint's tomb in the Collegiate Church.

## THE COMMON ROOM

The Common Room of the Collegium Maius was the professors' daily meeting-place and served as a refectory and was also used for University assemblies. Its original modest furnishings consisted only of tables and benches around the walls, but in 1468 an altar dedicated to St. Leonard was erected in the oriel window for the use of the lector. In 1428, it was the duty of each professor, in the order in which they obtained their degrees, to read aloud during meals.

In the Common Room the professors sat at three tables in order of seniority. The fare was modest and consisted of a plain soup, meat, fish, a good portion of turnips and peas, and for dessert porridge or dumplings with poppy-seed and honey, and fruit. Food was washed down with water or beer, wine war a rarity. Rector Stanisław Biel "himself who liked social gatherings, seemly gaiety and unceremonious banquets", set up a fund for eleven annual dinners. On these occasions tables were decorated with flowers; wine was served and guests were invited from other colleges. By custom a poor bachelor or student was invited to sit, in the place which St. John of Kęty, revered for his saintly nature, used to occupy at one time. On feast days boys from the nearby St. Anne's School would amuse the serious scholars with songs and Christmas entertainments.

In a separate coffer in the Common Room, were kept money and jewellery probably belonging to the Collegium Maius' and not to the University as a whole.

## THE ASSEMBLY HALL

At the beginning of the 16th century architect Marek was putting the gables and roofs on the former Pęcherz house and it was probably at this time that the theologians' lectorium was built — a large corner room, two storeys high, with four windows.
A lectorium, used by the theological faculty and also called "aula" or assembly

room, had existed here before (since the 14th century) but it had been much smaller.

Around 1507, the new room was completed and seven benches were installed in it. Both because of its size and convenient situation and proximity to the staircase, the room soon became the University's assembly hall.

Information from the 16th century concerning the assembly hall or, as it was more frequently called, the theologians' lectorium, is scanty. The hall was presumably furnished very modestly at that time. An entry from 1510 mentions a benchlike desk used by bachelors of theology. These are Jan Śniadecki's recollections of the old assembly hall in the 18th century:

"All commencement ceremonies, elections and public events took place with the

Bay window in the Common Room. In the back, a replica of a 14th-century statuette of Casimir the Great

The Common Room served not only as dining hall but also for professors' meetings. Today, the election of the Rector and receptions held by the University for distinguished visitors also take place there. In the back of the room, a Gdańsk staircase from the early 18th century

greatest pomp in the beautiful Jagiellonian Room, hung with large portraits of royal founders, benefactors and men famous for their knowledge or for services rendered to the Academy. Beneath the portraits, the walls were covered with crimson damask; the professors sat on elevated benches ranged round the walls of the room and covered with splendid Persian or Turkish rugs".

Of these furnishings very little has sur-

Two dining halls: in the Collegium Maius and in Bologna's Collegio di Spagna. The Bologna hall has a Gothic vault and the Cracow hall a beam ceiling. In spite of the differences, there is a similarity between the two halls, resulting above all from their function and furnishings

51

The north corner of the assembly hall. The Renaissance frieze bears the crests of professor; below are the music balcony, portraits, the Renaissance portal and the professors' benches

vived to our day. The frieze below the ceiling is, for the most part, a reconstruction painted by Zdzisław Pabisiak making use of surviving fragments whose style indicates a 16th century origin.

The conferring of academic degrees followed a ceremonial that still has not changed much. Professors in gowns sat on the benches and the Rector in a crimson gown was seated in the middle, in the Rector's chair which no one else was allowed to occupy. The guests sat facing the Rector. The room was filled with spectators, relatives and friends of the candidate. When silence fell, the Promotor, i.e. the professor who was to confer the degree, entered the room, led by the beadles. Then the eldest beadle called out the name of the candidate, adding: "Bene et feliciter veniat!" — Let him enter well and happily! Only then was the candidate ushered into the room. The Promotor then read the theses of the dissertation and the act of conferment of the degree. He also made a speech in Latin and, in a later part of the ceremony, distributed prizes to diligent students.

On 28 February 1527, there took place the "Prima promotio in hac celebri Academia trium egregiorum doctorum in sacra medicina". The word-order here seems to indicate that this was the first conferment of degrees of doctors of medicine at the University. It also seems that previous commencement ceremonies were not held in the "aula" because the room was not yet ready. This ceremony in the assembly hall was therefore considered an important event and was entered in the book of resolutions with the remark that this was done in case the events recorded were unknown to posterity: "ut posteritati non manifestus sit".

Here is the text of the entry:

"During the term of office of His Magnificence, Rector Łukasz of Nosków, doctor of liberal arts and medicine, lector ordinarus in medicine, physician and councillor to His Majesty the King, and Rector of our famous school in Cracow, in the years 1527, on the last day of February which fell on a Thursday, the following three illustrious doctors and masters of liberal arts obtained promotion and the degree of doctor of sacred medicine:

The Renaissance portal from the so-called Common Room of the former Cracow Town Hall (c. 1570) and the decorated inlaid door (c. 1600) — now in the assembly hall of the Collegium Maius

The frieze around the assembly hall is, for the most part, a reconstruction painted by Z. Pabisiak and based on preserved fragments

General view of the assembly hall, also called the Jagiellonian Room

The frieze around the assembly hall is, for the most part, a reconstruction painted by Z. Pabisiak and based on preserved fragments

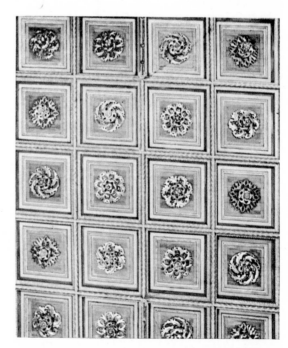

The Renaissance coffered ceiling in the assembly hall has a different rosette in every coffer. These were luckily preserved despite the changes of the 19th century. The beams, on the other hand, are reconstructions

Adam of Brzeziny, Mikołaj Sokolnicki and Szymon of Szamotuły".

After the promotion, the newly-created doctors were summoned to the desk to receive the doctor's insignia. This was performed with the following words : "By virtue of the privileges of our Academy, you are hereby handed the following insignia : first the book, and secondly — the cap and stole, the golden ring, a kiss with the teacher's blessing, and other objects...".

A similar description of a commencement ceremony is given by Maricius in his work "On the Academies". We shall return to this subject when describing present-day customs.

54

The assembly hall is the scene of many solemn occasions, including degree ceremonies and scientific sessions

## THE LIBRARY

It is not our purpose to present the history of the University library in the Collegium Maius which could fill more than one volume. On the other hand, one can hardly refrain from giving a description of the Library, as it emerges from archival material and University mementoes. The library room, the main home of the University collections was a long, L-shaped room lighted by membrane windows.

Glass windows were probably not installed until the 17th century.

Access to the library was through a gilded portal, more ornate than any other in Cracow, even including church portals. It is described in the chapter dealing with the building of Collegium Maius and its history.

Above the "porta aurea" is a balcony. Behind it, inside the library, probably on a wooden gallery, stood the mechanism of a clock striking the hours. Since this clock quite often went wrong, the beginning of lectures and classes was usually announced by a beadle ringing a hand bell from the balcony, which could be entered from the library.

The four ribs of the Gothic vault, over the library were of a span unknown in Cracow's profane buildings. In the 16th century, the vault already was painted blue, like those of the University libraries in Buda and Salamanca. The structure and colour of the vault were intended to symbolize the sky, or superior sphere, to which leads the road of knowledge contained in books.

In the centre of the room there were tables and by the windows, reading-desks. Monastic austerity prevailed, the furniture was simple, made of soft wood and not ornately sculptured as in the Laurentiana library in Florence.

Books were laid out on tables and desks, and secured with chains. This custom prevailed in the library until the middle of the 17th century. Donors would stipulate: "After my death, the book shall be attached by an iron chain in the artists' libraria and shall not be given out privately to anyone, so that it may not be lost". We also encounter many entries recording purchases of chains (1516, 1561, 1572, 1581, 1608, 1636).

In 1566, a book called *The Logical Circle* was secured with a golden chain. At the beginning of the 17th century, 28 padlocks were brought from Nysa and for the sake of convenience they were all opened with one key.

We find frequent evidence of care for the appearance of the books and for their uniform binding.

In 1563, a bronze bookbinder's seal with the arms of the University was acquired

The entrance to the Libraria, now the Senate conference room. On the wall is the University's large foundation painting. The vault is neo-Gothic and the furniture dates from the middle of the 19th century

to stamp the bindings. It is known today as the "super ex-libris" and bears the inscription *Librariae Collegii Maioris Cracoviensis*.

In 1578, sixteen locked bookcases were installed. Books were arranged in order of acquisition, whether by purchase or by donation. When gifts became very numerous, books were piled on the floor, which, however, proved unpractical. In the drawers of tables or desks were kept documents relating to the incomes of the University which had to be constantly available. Some silverware and objects of value used at anniversary masses for deceased benefactors (the chalice of Jan from Sandomierz, and the mitre and crosier of Abbot Jan Ponętowski) were also kept in the library, as were some of the

At present in the Libraria sessions of the academic Senate are held. The most important decisions concerning the University, its development and direction of research are therefore made in this room. Scientific sessions, seminars and classes are also, often held there

During the Swedish occupation in the years 1655—57, the University was forced to make various contributions. In this painting of 1820, Michał Stachowicz shows the looting of the library of Collegium Maius

rugs, paintings and portraits. Maps, skeletons, architectural models, engravings and instruments filled the bookcases. From the 16th century, medieval codices were giving way to printed books, and there were more and more items of furniture. Towards the end of the 17th century the interior of the library with its interesting collection of books, prints and other treasures must have made a picturesque impression. The keepers showed manuscripts, prints and curiosities to interested visitors and such visits soon became customary. Monarchs and diplomats visiting the Collegium showed interest in the library and the most interesting account of such a visit is that by the Frenchman Laboureure from the 17th century. He noted, among other things, that "the door to the library is of iron and the interior has bookcases all around and is full of reading desks to which books are chained so that they may not be taken away". The commendations of Papal nuncios like J. F. Commendoni and Ippolito Aldobrandini (who later became Pope Clement VIII) shows that the library must have been impressive even to Italians, well acquainted with collections of this kind.

In the 18th century, the library was thus described by Professor Józef Putanowicz: "In the Major College there is a magnificent library. It is estimated to have several thousand books in *omnibus facultatibus* and in material of various kinds. But these are nearly all by old authors and were donated by Benedictus a Koźmin, Ośliński, Makowski, and others — as professors are also doing today, from their own purse. Newer authors, and especially present-day ones, are lacking altogether, and yet they too are an element of the learned world..."

As has already been said, towards the

end of the 18th century the Collegium Maius lost its position as the main seat of the University and perhaps would even have been demolished, had it not been for the library growing within its walls. After the Kołłątaj reform, the Jagiello-

A view of the Libraria, now serving as the Senate room. For their deliberations members of the Senate sit at two long tables

The Libraria was different in the 19th century, when it served as the main storeroom of the Jagiellonian Library, having neo-Gothic stucco decorations, shelves and showcases

nian Library — as it began to be called then — grew considerably. Only partly linked to the library were the University Archives which were of great legal importance. In the 18th century, the Archives were transferred to a separate room on the ground floor.

Hardly any Polish institution (probably none apart from ecclesiastical institutions) can boast of such rich and so well preserved archives relating to its past. As early as the beginning of the 16th century, Rector Marcin Miechowita ordered the original resolutions from the years 1441—1505, as well as later ones, to be copied in one volume, which has luckily survived to this day.

In the 18th century, several attempts were made to put the archives in order, not so much out of historical curiosity but rather to put in order the rights and incomes of the University. In this respect much was owed to Kołłątaj.

Wrote Jan Śniadecki :

"The archives of the Cracow Academy which were later put in order and described by Józef Januszkiewicz, professor of State law, were formerly scattered in

In the 19th century, the library which was administered by energetic directors who were at the same time distinguished scholars (Jerzy Bandtkie, Józef Muczkowski, Karol Estreicher Sr.), gradually expanded over the entire building so that the whole Collegium was filled with books.

## THE DORMITORIES

As early as the beginning of the 15th century homes were organized for the students so that they were not forced to seek accomodation in the city, outside the University precincts. These dormitories were under the protection of the University, governed by its laws and administer-

The *Super Ex-libris* of the Collegium Maius Library. This sign was embossed on book bindings

various places, but were brought together by Kołłątaj ; having separated the University's privileges, laws and grants, he began to print them in chronological order. In the preface to this work, he intended to describe the history of learning in Poland and of the Cracow Academy from its foundation by Casimir the Great to our own times".

The oldest University hostel was the Jerusalem, founded by Chancellor Oleśnicki in 1456. We know its original appearance from the foundation tablet in the Collegium Maius

ed by seniors appointed by the Rector. The financial means of the dormitories varied and on the whole, were not sufficient to keep large numbers of students, even as late as the 19th century.

The two oldest were the Philosophers' Dormitory in Gołębia Street (at the corner occupied today by the Collegium Novum, opposite the garden of the Collegium Maius) and the Isner Dormitory, also called Pauperum (at present Wiślna Street). The University was indebted for both these dormitories to professors from Bohemia who came to Cracow in 1400. Mikołaj Isner from Prague, a distinguished scholar and educator, established his dormitory in 1409 for poor youth from

Later the Philosophers' dormitory, also called Bishop Noskowski's dormitory, was merged with the famous Jerusalem dormitory, founded by Cardinal Zbigniew Oleśnicki which was erected next-door to it in the years 1453—1456. The latter dormitory was probably so named after the owner, rather than — as legend has it — in connection with the bishop's vow — not fulfilled — that he would make a pilgrimage to Jerusalem. Both dormitories were consumed by fire in 1841 but the ruins were not pulled down until 40 years later to make room for the Collegium Novum. The two dormitories accommodated about 150 students.

The Długosz (or Canonists') dormitory has

In the 19th century, the Jerusalem dormitory resembled a burgher's mansion; next to it stood the so-called New dormitory. Poor students lived in a hostel especially founded for them in 1409, at the corner of Wiślna and Gołębia Street. All these dormitories were demolished in the 19th century

Lithuania and Ruthenia. The dormitory was later enlarged several times with gifts from various benefactors (Długosz, Anna Jagiellon) so that it eventually lodged 200 students. Those better-off occupied front rooms on the ground floor, while the poorer ones lived in the annexe.

not survived to our times; it was demolished in 1844. It was situated in Grodzka Street, next to St. Peter's Church, opposite the Collegium Iuridicum and lodged about 100 students.

In the 15th and 16th centuries there were also the Grochowa dormitory in Kanonicza Street, the Hungarian dormitory in Bracka Street, and the German dormitory — later called New — in the garden of the Collegium Maius. It seems that there existed a dormitory for medical students (in Grodzka Street ?) and a Czech dormitory. On the whole it appears that both students and junior professors (extranei) had plentiful accommodation in Cracow, especially if we take into account the possibility of finding private quarters in town or residing in monasteries — to which the University authorities approved reluctantly.

The same laws and customs were in force in all dormitories. The inmates were divided into servitors, gracialists and extranei. The former attended to the professors and for this were given bed and board. The gracialists had only accomodation. The extranei were graduates who were what we would today call assistants. The dormitories were furnished modestly. As a rule, the common room on the upper floor served as a chapel, and beyond this came crowded sleeping quarters. The kitchen was one of the most important parts of the house. We happen to know the inventory of utensils belonging to the Hungarians who, in 1557, left their effects for safe-keeping to a certain medical student. Their belongings were extremely modest and consisted of one copper pot, two frying pans, eight pewter plates, two pewter jugs, one salt-cellar, one dish-cloth, one wash-bowl, two wooden bowls, one table, one small table, one money-box, two padlocks, the book of laws, the privilege of drawing salt (from 1510), Peter the Spaniard's Dialectics, Aristotle's Priora, Peter Helio's Grammar, the Book of the Soul, one map (old and black).

This, however, is an example of poverty. The Jerusalem or Lawyers' dormitory was richer. It also had its own well stocked library. Jan Kanty Steczkowski left behind a detailed description of customs in force in the Jerusalem Dormitory in the early 19th century:

"Admission to the dormitory depended on the senior and had to be approved by the Rector of the Jagiellonian University ; at that time Walenty Litwiński was the Rector. The admission fee of 6 zlotys was paid to the senior and then one could live in the dormitory without paying anything

The Law-students' Dormitory, founded by Jan Długosz, was in Gołębia Street, opposite the Collegium Iuridicum. Destroyed by a fire in the middle of the 19th century, it shared the fate of the other hostels

until graduation from secondary school and even until University graduation, provided, of course, that one's conduct was quiet and moral. Sometimes even wealthy parents would send their sons to a dormitory if there were vacancies, in order to keep them under closer supervision.

"In the spacious corridor every student living in the dormitory had a simple chest where he kept his provisions. Once a week, or at somewhat longer intervals, his parents or guardians would send him bread, cheese, butter, bacon, flour, various cereals, potatotes and whatever else God would allow and the parents could send or bring. In this way, every student kept house for himself for the week or even longer, and he had to be a good manager in order to make his supplies last until the next expected parcel from home — or else he had to pull in his stomach.

"In the kitchen, there were iron grates set up along the length of the big hearth, heaped with fire-wood and coal. Each student brought to the kitchen in a pot marked with his initials whatever his pantry would allow ; only one pot, how-

61

This woodcut from the collections of the Jagiellonian Library shows a professor at his desk and students seated on low benches during a lecture

ever, because there was no room for two, let alone for more, since in the same kitchen and on the same fire, food was cooked for the whole household of the senior. For this reason broth and different soups were not known in the dormi-

tory ; a student who could afford to spend a few pennies would go to the butcher's stall himself and buy half a pound of meat ; then, in order to take no more than one small pot to the kitchen, he would usually add some barley porridge to it, and thus he had barley soup.

"Living in the dormitory was very convenient, especially for the poor students, because of the proximity of the school. Indeed, even in foulest weather, snow blizzard or hard frost, the students, after leaving the dormitory, had only to cross a small courtyard to enter the long cor-

A 16th-century Cracow woodcut showing scholars marking the course of a comet on a globe, with the help of an astrolabe and a turquetum

Lectures also took place in the assembly hall. The professor would usually sit on the stone benches by the window

ridor under the library in the Collegium Maius which led to the library courtyard — and then they were under a roof again."

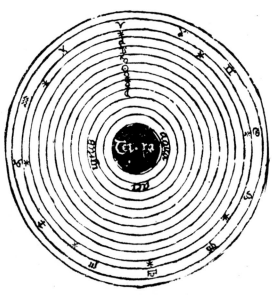

Preserved in the collections of the Jagiellonian University's Museum is this original 15th-century woodcut block representing the celestial spheres and the course of the planets round the earth. We see the earth (terra), the sphere of water (aqua), air (aer) and fire (ignis), according to the Ptolemaic system taught at the University

## TUITION

We have touched on various aspects of University life. It is now time to speak of the most important sphere of activity, namely that of tuition.

In nearly all medieval Universities, appointments to chairs were made according to seniority and not to specialization. In Cracow this system prevailed, with minor changes, until the Kołłątaj reform in the 18th century.

Textbooks, commentaries, summaries of lectures from all periods, have been preserved in the Jagiellonian Library. These records give us a glimpse of teaching methods, but it is more difficult to get to know the process of instruction itself, the student's ordinary day, the way the lecture or "lesson", proceeded, the kind

The ground-floor reading-room beneath the Libraria where lectures took place in the Middle Ages. The paintings on the vaulted ceiling date from the late 16th century. Ballistics, architecture, mechanics are among the subjects depicted (16th—17th cent.) on the walls of the Aristotle Lectorium

of questions put or answers received, the methods maintaining discipline, etc.

The lectoria in the Collegium Maius were named Galenus, Socrates, Maro, Archimedes and Plato after the famous scholars of antiquity. These names have been

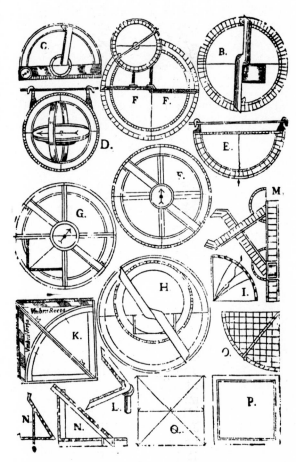

The Galenus Lectorium, where at one time lectures were also held, now houses the archeological collections of the Jagiellonian University's Museum

retained to the present day. The theology students had their lectures in the assembly hall on the 1st floor where weekly disputations were also held.

Like Bologna's Collegio di Spagna, the Collegium Maius had (since 1467 ?) a clock which struck the hours, thus announcing the beginning and the end of lectures. There still remains the balcony over the entrance to the library where this clock once stood. Unfortunately the mechanism broke down often, exposing the University to radicule. In 1522, Rector Maciej Miechowita "at a meeting of the Professors offered 130 ducats for installing a new clock with figures, the phases of

the sun and moon, and a hand showing the hours".

In the olden days, (up to the 18th century), the start of the University day was determined by the season and the hours of day light. The class-rooms and lectoria were dark and anyone with poor eyesight was at a considerable disadvantage. Teachers and students sat near the windows where the light was best. At first, there were no permanent benches in the lectoria and the students would bring with them small stools placed in a cluster near the professor. In winter and autumn, all wore their warmest clothes because there was an icy draught from the windows. The professor sat by the window in a fur-coat (if he had come to acquire

Among the medieval hand-written or printed textbooks there are some dealing with the use of astrolabes. Here is a woodcut from "De usu astrolabii"

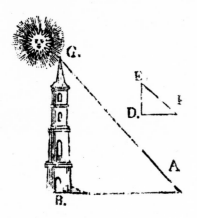

Woodcut representing the principles of triangulation, preserved in the collections of the Jagiellonian University's Museum

cordance with fixed principles; in disputationes the students were questioned and helped to produce traditionally accepted answers; in sermones the students had to deliver sermon-like speeches. (This latter form was practised chiefly in theological studies).

Armillary shperes, astronomical eclipses, trigonometric angles and figures and the Pythagorean theorem, are among the interesting mathematical figures painted on the wall of the Aristotle Lectorium. They probably date from the 17th century

one). When it was quite dark, a candle or oil-lamp was lit.

In the lecture rooms there were blackboards, probably very similar to those used today; painted on the wall or on a board were the letters of the alphabet (in Greek or Hebrew), mathematical formulae, plans, maps and symbols.

In the 15th century, students made notes on their slates with chalk or slate pencils, or on wax-coated plates. Also known were quills or sharpened reeds, silver or lead pencils, crayons, chalk and ink. Students carried their books and slates in small bags.

In the arts faculty, which provided preparatory courses for studies in other faculties, a selected work by some author was studied through the winter and summer term. In the faculties of law and medicine, not to mention the faculty of theology, a lecture or commentary, or commentary to a commentary, sometimes dragged on for several years.

As a rule the lectures were based on the writings of one particular author. Thus until the 18th century philosophy was based on the works of Aristotle. The professors commented on the work studied but did not expound his own views. The teaching of Philosophy and law as well as theology was thus based on the recapitulation of outdated theories.

Instruction was made up of three elements: *lectiones, disputationes* and *sermones*. In lectiones the teacher read part of a book and commented on it in ac-

This combination of lecture and instruction based on a set text was a most disastrous method which eventually reduced the University in the 17th and 18th centuries to the level of a secondary school. It was perhaps not so bad, when applied to speculative disciplines such as philosophy or theology, or to law, where the book of decrees served as the basis for the lecture and disputations; nor was it so disastrous when in the 16th and 17th centuries it produced highflown commentaries on classical writers. The real harm was done when this system based on treatises, dogmas and canons was applied to the natural sciences, mainly to medi-

65

The so-called Long Vestibule, with 16th-century paintings

cine, but also to astronomy, chemistry, physics, zoology and geography. This left the field wide open for flights of fantasy and to occult practices.

Before sitting for an examination, the student had to show that he had participated in a certain number of disputations which, as a rule, were not popular. The first degree was the baccalaureate, the second was a master's or doctor's degree. These degrees gave the right to teach. Examinations conferred no other rights (except the right to attend patients for those who held medical degrees).

Yet life proved stronger than superstition and the Copernican theory gained ground in the end although the Ptolemaic system was binding in Cracow until the second half of the 18th century, as the only one consistent with the teaching of the Church.

From the 16th century, discipline slackened. Studies could be persued without examinations and there was no dividing line between regular and extra-mural students. To many, the University became

a school for acquiring a general culture. Actually, the sons of the gentry needed no professional education to make a start in life.

At the beginning of the 17th century, the antiquated system of tuition was somewhat improved and lectures became less haphazard after the practice of drawing lots in order to select the professors who were to give certain classes was put a stop to. The number of Aristotelian classes and unpopular disputations, was also reduced.

Instruction was given in Latin but in practice the vernacular gradually prevailed because it was not until they entered the University that students acquired a knowledge of foreign languages. German was never used very much in the Collegium but Latin was widespread. When in 1787 Śniadecki began lecturing on algebra in Polish, older professors were very much surprised.

A University career was not an easy one. It usually started with the post of auxiliary teacher, the so-called minor colleague who taught mathematics and geometry, grammar and the ABC of logic. When a chair in the Collegium Maius, maintained from royal grants, became vacant, a minor colleague could be appointed to it.

Apart from professors or "masters", there were their numerous assistants — bachelors, extranei professors or licentiates, who were attached to colleges but lectured only as substitutes or taught elsewhere, e.g. in dormitories. For the most part they taught without remuneration while waiting for an opening — or lived by private lessons and then were dependent on their pupils. It was they who caused the Rectors most trouble; the fault lay in the organization of the University, which failed to ensure an adequate income and position to young people with a zeal for learning.

## THE RESIDENTS

The professors were greatly attached to the Collegium in which they lived and worked. They would bequeath their personal properties to the University and, in the College annals, warm obituaries were in turn devoted to them. Here is an ex-

Jan Brożek (1585—1652), astronomer and mathematician ; one of the most illustrious professors of the first half of the 17th century, was a fervent champion of the University's rights against the encroaching Jesuits. He was also a fervent supporter of the teaching of Copernicus, and kept alive his memory by assembling Copernican mementos in the Collegium Maius. An eminent scholar himself, Jan Brożek corresponded with great mathematicians and astronomers, including Galileo. He bequeathed his scientific instruments to the University and his memory has remained alive to this day. His portrait, reproduced above, was hung according to his wish in the Common Room, in the place of honour

The south entrance from the galleries to the professors' lodgings on the 2nd floor, was built around 1500. The wall of rough-hewn stone is part of the former Pęcherz house from the 14th century

safely. He was a sociable man and enjoyed suitable convivial gatherings with friends. To the end of his days, he endeavoured to maintain a serene countenance and peace of mind, even at times of dejection. He was a great lover of our Collegium and proved it by his deeds. Indeed, when old age took away his strength and when, weakened by age rather than by illness, he rested his head on his hands and went to join his Maker — which happened on the 27th day of August 1541 — even then he performed an act of very great generosity to us; he donated 200 florins for the reconstruction of the damaged corner of the Collegium, and 600 florins for founding an altar in the common room. He also offered to the Assembly two bowls and two tumblers marked with his initials, as well as six big spoons."

The professors' lodgings were furnished and equipped at the same time as the

Window with window seat in the room of Professor Żołędziowski

ample of such an obituary from 1541, touching in its simplicity and Renaissance charm:

"The venerable master Stanisław Biel of Nowe Miasto, doctor of sacred theology from the age of thirty-eight, and canon of Cracow from the age of twenty-one, remains dear to our memory as a true Abraham of our University. He was a wealthy man and reached a great old age, maybe as much as 83 years. He won wide fame. From childhood he lived in chastity. When he obtained his master's degree he travelled to Rome. He studied at the Universities of Cologne, Leipzig, Frankfort and other cities, and returned

The room of Ambroży Grabowski, bookseller and distinguished historian of Cracow, is furnished with his own furniture. Grabowski, while not a professor himself, lived in close friendship with such greeat scholars as Przybylski, Ossoliński, Bandtkie, and exerted influence on a number of 19th-century historians, especially in the field of art history

Professor Żołędziowski's room is furnished with peasant furniture and a 16th-century tapestry. Old inventories contain descriptions of this kind of furniture in professors' lodgings. Żołędziowski was a professor in the 18th century

halls and common rooms. From the 15th but mainly from the 16th century, the records of the Collegium contain many entries concerning the professors' lodgings. The latter deserve special attention since they then acquired an appearance that remained unchanged for three hundred years. We know numerous inventories of these apartments drawn up when they were vacated by one of their tenants. There were three lodgings on the ground floor of the building: one beneath the Common Room, and two opposite St. Anne's Church. The other lodgings were on the 1st and 2nd floor. Most of the lodgings were on two floors. Wooden stairs led from the first-floor rooms, through the ceiling, to the upper floor. This layout has not survived to our day. The furnishings of the apartments were modest. Inventories list a few religious paintings, books and painted furniture. Exceptionally we find in professors' lodgings paintings with such subjects as "Solomon's Judgment" or "The Virtuous Susannah".

Not only the professors' savings but also their personal belongings and furniture became the property of the Collegium (unless other instructions were left in the will) and enriched its collections (e.g. Petrarca's portrait from the apartment of Professor Krzysztof Sowiński, 1699). The last member of the College to live in the Collegium Maius was Professor Józef Bogucicki, a distinguished professor of ecclesiastical history.

When the apartment passed to a new tenant a detailed inventory was made by the administrator of the Collegium, assisted by witnesses. In the records there are no accounts of serious disputes over the allocation of lodgings, which changed hands in a friendly and courteous atmosphere: "The Most Venerable Piotr Praclewicz, professor of sacred theology, took possession of the apartment assigned to him and situated next to the library. May it bring to this gentleman happiness and success. These are the heartfelt wishes of Master Marcin Bielecki, at this time praepostor of the Major College, appearing here as witness". Or: "May this apartment serve Master Kasper Benedykt Kowalczewski for a long time and happily, and may Heaven receive him from here in his very old age...".

Here are two inventories, from 1617 and

1724 respectively, which give an idea how the lodgings were furnished: "The residence above the Socrates lectorium was handed over to the worthy gentleman Sigonius, professor of theology, on 13 December 1617, after the death of Sieradzki, professor of theology, incumbent of St. Florian's. Upper room (on the 2nd floor): one carved table with a drawer, shelves on all sides, one wardrobe for clothes, another table, old, with carved flower patterns, two reading-desks, one jug from the washroom iron doors and

"Here is Benedykt of Koźmin who added income and books to your possessions, Oh Library" — this inscription under the portrait painted around 1540 is an expression of gratitude to the University's distinguished professor and benefactor. The portrait is an outstanding Polish Renaissance painting

A student's writing-desk from the 18th century, an inkstand from the 17th century, and an oil lamp from the middle of the 19th century — mementos of former residents of the Collegium Maius

windows in good condition; a cupboard in the vestibule.

"Lower room (on the 1st floor): a cupboard by the door with lock and keys, another by the window with locks and keys; old wall shelves; windows in good condition; two benches; two tables — keys for all the doors of the apartment; one table-cloth".

In 1724, Professor Marcin Kurowski took over the apartment on the St. Anne's Street side: "All rooms were found refurbished and in good condition, with two good stoves, all windows in good condition, with doors, locks, keys.

"Hanging in the first room or vestibule are pictures of the 12 Apostles, all painted in a similar manner. A small painting of the Crucifixion. In the same room there are wall hangings, not in good condition however, and three painted benches. In the larger central room — a painting of the Saviour, a good table on lathe-turned legs, and a cupboard in good condition for keeping vessels and jugs. The windows are double.

"Next comes the dining room. Hanging here is a painting of St. Jerome, a table and a small cupboard. In the last room

Alojzy Putanowicz was a professor and historian in the times prior to the Kołłątaj reform and left behind an excellent description of the University. He appears here in the Rector's gown with ermine tippet, after 18th-century fashion

Portrait of Antoni Żołędziowski, a jurist who in the middle of the 18th century represented the interests of the University in Rome. It was painted by Tadeusz Konicz, an artist active in Rome at that time

is a painting representing Jakub Witeliusz, Canon of Cracow. The bookcase contains books. In the upper part of the apartment, to which there is access by stairs, there is one good window, a floor of bricks, one painting and one old and worn-out carpet.

"In the vestibule, there is an iron door, a green-painted wardrobe, a wash-stand, and an iron sheet in front of the stove. In the servant's room there is a small table."

This is how modestly and austerely, poorly in fact — lived the collegiate academicians, as professors were called in Cracow. Apart from the professors, their servants, i.e. the boys attending to them, and the door-keepers also lived in the Collegium. The latter had even more modest accommodation, usually in some cubby-holes.

The Collegium was always watched by a dog. One such dog appears in a 19th-century view of the Collegium Maius courtyard, painted by Antoni Brodowski, and in the recollections of J. K. Turski: "Among our friends — especially as we passed St. Anne's Street in the morning — was a big shaggy black dog called Negro. Negro would follow every student in whose packet he scented a roll or piece of bread ... Negro would smell out everything and he demanded excise on everything. It could not be helped — you had to pay ransom. Yet we liked this fine and playful dog. It was fun to watch how he would sometimes assail a small sprat: he would get on his hind legs when he was much taller than the little lad and would bark until the scared boy threw all his bread to him".

Sebastian Petrycy (1554—1626), a physician, was the author of instructions on how to behave during plague epidemics. He also wrote poetry, translated David's Psalms and Horace's Carmina

Szymon Starowolski (1588—1656) was one of the most distinguished professors in the 17th century. He left behind historical works which have retained their value to the present day. The portrait, a copy of an unknown original, shows him against the tomb of King Ladislas Łokietek

## CELIBACY

The residents of the Collegium — major colleagues as they called themselves — were obliged to be conscious at all times of the dignity of their position and of the House. There existed severe rules concerning their behaviour, dress, order, work and conversations with women. Misdemeanour, brawls and insults were all punished.

It is not easy to give an answer to the question whether all professors were obliged to observe celibacy. This varied and depended on circumstances. Although in principle only unmarried professors were allowed to reside in college some professors could be married. Thus Mikołaj from Koprzywnica, administrator of the Collegium for many years at the turn of the 15th/16th century, was married by special Papal permission. Also married was Walenty Fontana, the distinguished professor of medicine (and mathematician at the same time), deceased in 1618. Professors of medicine were often married men; indeed, it was improper for clergymen to be physicians, let alone surgeons. As late as the 18th century, Kołłątaj had to try to obtain a release from monastic vows for Professor Rafał Czerwiakowski, a distinguished surgeon; Kołłątaj argued that it was unbecoming for a monk to give medical assistance as surgeon and obstetrician.

In 1610, Professor Romer from Stężyca demanded that married professors be dismissed from the University. This apparently did not take place since twenty years later Jakub Najmanowicz wrote of those professors "who in old age get married to young women, on any occasion, at any first sign, and whoever she gets hold of, she will at once complain, just

Józef Dietl (1804—1878), physician and professor of medicine, fought for the use of the vernacular at the University at the time of Austrian oppression. He was also a distinguished mayor of Cracow. In this portrait by Jan Matejko, Dietl is wearing a dean's gown

sake of dignity. Kołłątaj was a clergyman himself. It is true, however, that while stressing his loyal attitude towards the Church, he followed secular fashions —

Sigismund III giving the mace to the University in the Wawel Castle — a painting by Michał Stachowicz (1820). The professors are wearing 18th century gowns

to bother the poor old man, and to stir up things with her womanly whims and babbling — without reckoning whether it be good or bad, whether there be any sense to it or not..."

Another thing is that some professors, and especially the younger ones, often lived in illegal unions, which is mentioned in Rector's judgements. Such liaisons were looked upon with some tolerance, but everything was done to suppress quarrels between women living in the vicinity of colleges or dormitories — which, of course, was not an easy matter. In St. Anne's Street, one could often hear the angry shouts of quarrelling women.

At the time of Kołłątaj's reform most professors were still clergymen. It was considered for a long time that a university teacher, had to be a priest and subject to ecclesiastical jurisdiction, if only for the

In 1851, during the Emperor Francis Joseph's visit to the University, the professors refused to appear in Austrian official uniforms. It was reluctantly agreed that they should wear gowns

In the course of the 19th century, the Rector's attire assumed the form, which it has at present: a crimson gown with a large collar and ermine tippet called mucet and a red cap. The Rector wears the chain and a signet ring on his right hand. It is in such attire that Rector Józef Dietl appears on the portrait by J. Hruzik.

which in fact, caused him trouble and lawsuits (a case concerning his short costume and bright stockings).

The professors were usually ordained late in life, mainly in order to obtain well-paid chairs of theology. This explains the absence of excessive devoutness among the professors and, especially in the period of the counter-reformation, a certain independence of opinions.

The bishops of Cracow and the Jesuits supported by them were never popular at the University, because professors (even if they might not be very distinguished scholars) felt they were not dependent on the ecclesiastical or monastic hierarchy.

The secular status of the University excepting the theological faculty dates from 1809 when, after the incorporation of Cracow into the Duchy of Warsaw, four faculties were organized anew. In the 19th century, the number of clergymen teaching secular subjects gradually decreased. One of the exceptions was father Stefan Pawlicki, the distinguished historian and philologist (d. 1916) who occupied the chair of history of philosophy.

## THE GOWNS

The professors, called masters or doctors, once wore gowns and caps in accordance with the customs prevailing in medieval universities. The students, called scholars, also had to wear gowns. Such academic dress has survived to our day in some English universities.

The gowns varied. At first, in the 15th century, they were simple and resembled a monks' habit with a cowl but in time they became more and more sumptuous. We know the gown of St. John of Kęty from the 15th century, which is a simple habit in a grey-green woollen fabric. The University Museum also preserves the tippet (or "mucet") of the Rector's gown and a cap, part of the same costume from the 18th century, which is believed to have been Kołłątaj's gift to Jan Śniadecki. The tippet is of white satin, richly braided with gold, and in the back it folds to form a cowl.

In 1660, Master Wierzbicki donated a new crimson gown of costly cloth to be worn by his dean and in return the University

Senate granted him the right to wear a gown at all academic disputations, and recorded this decision for the posterity, to be read, repeated and imitated.

The professors' gowns and caps did not retain the same cut throughout history. In the 16th century, gowns were ample and, according to the humanist fashion, had wide sleeves; the cap was flat and soft. In the 17th century, velvet tippets were added to gowns after the Italian fashion. In the 18th century, gowns began to be trimmed with gold braid.

The professors' gowns were the target of much teasing especially the tippets which in front hung loose like bibs or napkins. It was said that "professors wear on their shoulders wise Aristotelian pants" to cover their ignorance, and that they cared more for income-bringing gowns than for lessons. We encounter such censure in the 17th century (coming from Jesuit

An 1821 etching by Michał Stachowicz shows a ceremonial procession entering the Jagiellonian Room

In 1584, a banquet was given in honour of Queen Anna Jagiellon. Painting by Michał Stachowicz (1821)

circles) and in the 18th century. This might be the reason why gowns went out of fashion after 1809 and were not reverted to (except for beadles); they were not considered dignified and even ridiculous.

Ceremonial dress at that time was either a uniform with sword and cocked hat, or a frock-coat.

In 1851, in connection with a visit paid by the Emperor Francis Joseph, much thought was given to what dress the Professors should appear in the Collegium Maius. Since they did not want to wear official Austrian uniforms, they decided to revert to traditional attire. The cut and colour of today's gowns were adopted at this time; a red gown with ermine tippet for the Rector, and black gowns with velvet tippets of different colours for the professors of the various faculties (purple for theology, black for law, blue for philo-

Among the most valuable mementos is the armorial cartouche of Sigismund III from the time of his wedding with Queen Anne of Austria (1592)

Signature by Anna Jagiellon in the guest book of the Jagiellonian University (1584): "Anna Queen of Poland in her own hand"

sophy and red for medicine). The gowns are worn with square velvet caps.

Life proved stronger than regulations. The scholars could not be forced to wear at all times gowns with cowls like monks; the bachelors and masters preferred to do on lay dress. This can be seen from repeated Rector's orders and from the fines imposed.

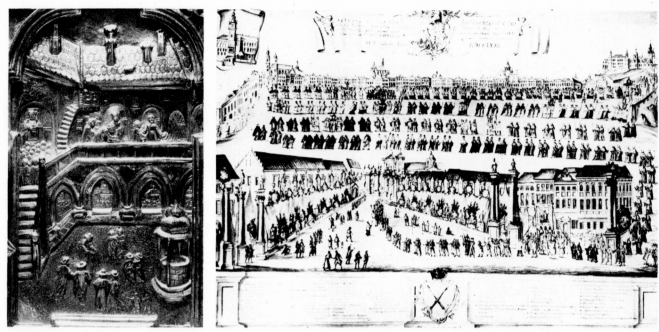

Bas-relief on the reliquary of St. John of Kęty with professors and students in the courtyard and in the background the lectoria with professors teaching. On the right is the roofed well. Solemn occassions are best portrayed in the scene of the grand University procession from the Wawel to the Collegium Maius (1775)

## PROCESSIONS AND RECEPTIONS

University processions derived from church processions and have, to some extent, retained that character to the present day. Above all, they have retained the *ordo canonicus*, i.e. the order of procession with the students marching first, followed by the professors, wearing gowns and lecturers according to faculties, then by the Senate and finally, the Rector. The faculty members and Rector are preceded by beadless carrying maces.

Marcin Radymiński, the 17th-century historiographer of the University, left behind a description of the procession held when the University was installed in the Collegium Maius in the year 1400; although it is a later account, it has a certain value for us because it is based on customs prevailing in Radymiński's times which had much older traditions behind them.

We could not possibly list here all the University processions of the past; in times when there was little public entertainment, processions — even if nothing but branches, flowers and wreaths were carried in the absence of other decorations — were very popular.

Among the most frequent festivities in which the University took a leading part (something the professors were always made sure of), were the royal entries to Cracow *). As a rule, the University welcomed the monarchs at Kleparz, at the entrance to the city or less frequently in St. Mary's Church, and the Rector would pronounce a lengthy oration. The historian Maciej Stryjkowski has left behind the following account of the welcoming of Henry de Valois (1574):

*As they entered the Market Square,*
*Trumpets and drums sounded*
*everywhere,*
*The King stepped into the Church*
*of Saint Mary,*
*And listened to the Collegiates' fine*
*oratory.*
*To greet the monarch in the Market*
*Square*

---

*) See : Henryk Barycz, *Historia Uniwersytetu Jagiellońskiego w epoce humanizmu* (History of the Jagiellonian University in the Age of Humanism), 1935.

Two royal signatures in the Jagiellonian University's guest book: Stephen Batory's (1575) and Sigismund III's (1588). They were decorated with drawings in order to stress the importance of the visit and of the signature

Of equally solemn character was the visit paid in 1684 by John III, after the victory of Vienna. The King's signature is surrounded by allegorical figures and emblems of chivalry. The signature of Queen Marie-Casimire was framed by a decorated portal

*A triumphal arch was erected there*
*To manifest gratitude and content*
*On this magnificent event.*

Professor Józef Sołtykowicz, the distinguished although now forgotten historian of the University, wrote in 1810 on the

precedence accorded to the University during festivities:

"At the public act in 1604, attended by Crown Prince Ladislas, the Nuncio Claudio Rangoni, the Bishop of Cracow Bernard Maciejowski, the Bishop of Kuyavia and Deputy Crown Chancellor Piotr Tylicki, the Grand Crown Marshal Zygmunt Myszkowski, and a great number of Senators — at this academic meeting, I say — Rector Mikołaj Dobroczeski sat between the Crown Prince and the Papal Nuncio, like the Rector of the Paris Academy who, on festive occasions, sat before the peers of the State and the nuncios, and in public processions marched side by side with the Metropolitan of Paris. During the coronation of Henry of Valois and the solemn procession to Skałka on that occasion, the Rector held in that memorable and splendid ceremony a higher place than the Chapter of the Cracow Cathedral — as history records it."

In 1578 the Papal Nuncio Caligari gave

The arms of Poland and Lithuania at the time of Stanislas Augustus, probably painted in 1787, when the King visited the University

78

the following account of the welcome given to him by the professors: "The Rector, doctors and scholars appeared in formal attire, with solemn pomp, in great numbers. I accorded them a formal audience in church, sitting on my stool behind the altar-rail, and they all stood in front of me bareheaded although I asked them to cover their heads, but in vain. Their oration was long and full of expressions of gratitude".

The University has to this day remained faithful to the tradition of welcoming ceremonies and assists the State and City authorities on such occasions.

The routes of processions varied. From the Wawel or from Kleparz, they led around Market Square, by St. Anne's and

The signature of Adam Naruszewicz, the distinguished historian, who accompanied Stanislas Augustus during the King's visit to the Jagiellonian University in 1787

Professors leaving the Libraria to attend the inauguration ceremony of a new academic year

Gołębia Streets, to the Collegium Novum or to the Collegium Iuridicum in Grodzka Street. The Collegium Maius was always decorated with greenery and garlands. In the courtyard gallery, rugs and tapestries were hung out. Thus in order to welcome John Sobieski III after the victory of Vienna (1683), the courtyard was decorated with rugs ; a receipt for the tapestries borrowed was given to the administrator of the Collegium Maius.

Professor Henryk Barycz wrote :

"Not always did the welcoming ceremonies go off without a hitch. In December 1605, when, after a prolonged wait, the coach with Archduchess Constance, the bride of Sigismund III, finally stopped in front of St. Florian's Church, and Rector Schoneus stepped out to make the welcoming speech, the horses became impatient and the carriage drove away, giving the Rector no chance to deliver his oration. Everybody therefore proceeded to the Castle and there Schoneus made his speech of homage in the presence of the mother, brother and sister of the Archduchess. Even worse was the experience of Rector Bazyli Golinjusz at the welcoming of Nuncio Gianbattista Lancellot in 1623. The Rector got so mixed up in his speech that, without finishing it, he quickly retired together with the masters accompanying him.

"The University appeared with particular pomp at royal funerals. According to the accepted custom, it had its permanent place assigned in the funeral procession, before the Chapter and the Episcopate. It is true that at the funeral of Queen Marie-Louise in September 1667 the City Council tried to take this place, but the masters did not allow the intruders to crowd into the pageant, so that the councillors had to walk on the other side of the street, and very soon, at Kanonicza Street, they slipped away altogether. Apart from masters and doctors, scholars also attended all funerals ; together with students from the higher schools, they usually appeared in long black robes and cowls, carrying candles."

From the times of Sigismund Augustus it became the custom for kings to visit the Collegium Maius and to be welcomed there by an oration after which they inspected the library and assembly hall. The librarian Mikołaj of Szadek left behind the following account of Sigismund Augustus' visit to the Collegium Maius in 1553 : "The King would not miss a visit to the Collegium Maius, that jewel of his ancestors. After his arrival, he inspected the Common Room and the lectoria, then he visited the library and examined the number of books and astronomical instruments."

Not forgotten to this day are the visits to the University of Anna Jagiellon in 1584, of John III with his wife and sons in 1684, and of Stanislas Augustus in 1787. The latter visit — indeed the last to be paid to the Collegium Maius by a King of Poland — was even commemorated by a plaque over the entrance to the assembly hall or Jagiellonian Room.

The most splendid University ceremony in the 18th century was the great procession held in 1776 on the occasion of the

Professors assembling in the courtyard for the grand Jubilee procession in 1964

canonization of St. John of Kęty. Engravings from the procession have been preserved and show that it was held in baroque style. Architect Franciszek Placidi decorated the Market Square with wooden altars, columns, triumphal arches, figures and emblems. St. Anne's Street

Preceded by a beadle carrying the mace, the Rector in gown, cap and chain is on his way to the inauguration ceremony of a new academic year

The academic Senate proceeding along Floriańska Street for the inauguration of the Jubilee festivities in 1964 (the 600th anniversary of the University's foundation). The street was decorated with the emblems of Cracow's higher schools and scientific institutions

was closed by a so-called "structure" representing the celestial triumph and the façades of houses were covered with screens of cloth on wooden frames. A slow-moving procession of the fraternities, clergy, schools and students, preceded the faculties and the Rector and crowds were gathered in the streets to welcome the University.

## THE COPERNICAN TRADITION

Copernicus became part of Cracow's university tradition although he had not been a professor there but only a student in the years 1491—1495. After his return from Italy to Warmia, where he settled from 1503 as the Canon of Frombork, Cracow scholars (Marcin Biem, Gabriel Prokopiades, Bernard Wapowski and J. Solfa) maintained contacts with him.

N·COPERNIC. n. a. 1473
E. a. 1543

Living in Cracow from the middle of the 16th century was Joachim Retyk, an outstanding pupil of Copernicus and publisher of the latter's monumental work. Thus the Copernican theories were surely known in Cracow in the 16th century and were even taught there (Walenty Fontana).

It was not until the 17th century that the Copernican discovery became accepted, first in the Protestant countries, where the heliocentric theory was not condemned so strongly as it had been by the Catholic Church.

In the 17th century Copernicus continued to be revered in Cracow. Two historians of the University, Szymon Starowolski and Marcin Radymiński, wrote his biography and in 1630 Jan Brożek, a distinguished professor of mathematics, travelled to Pomerania and Warmia in search of Copernican mementos. He brought to Cracow letters (unfortunately not preserved), his portrait and a portrait of Copernicus' father which is still in the University Museum; according to tradition this portrait (for a tombstone) was painted by the great astronomer himself, which is not unlikely.

On the occasion of a session held in honour of Copernicus, in Leipzig in 1742, Józef Aleksander Jabłonowski searched the Collegium Maius for Copernicas mementoes. He probably removed the portrait of Copernicus at this time. Later-on in 1766, he had a bust of Copernicus made in Cracow; which was to be sent to Toruń where Jabłonowski intended to erect a monument to the astronomer.

During the Englightenment, Śniadecki's speech on Copernicus, delivered in 1782, may be considered a turning point since the Church no longer persisted in its opposition to the Copernican theory.

In 1802 during the Austrian occupation, Jędrzej Śniadecki sent to the Scientific Society in Warsaw a comprehensive bio-

The portrait of Copernicus' father, Nicolas the elder, resembles the features of his son the astronomer. It is not an original but a copy from the tomb painting in Toruń. The copy was commissioned for the Collegium Maius by Jan Brożek. Apart from explanatory inscriptions, the coats of arms of the Copernicus family are placed in the four corners of the picture

graphy of Copernicus which was later translated into foreign languages. In 1821, Rector Sebastian Sierakowski erected a monument to Copernicus in the Collegiate Church of St. Anne.

There are many portraits of Nicolas Copernicus and a number of works devoted to them. There is much to indicate that the small portrait preserved at the Jagiellonian University is a copy of a self-portrait made by Copernicus himself. In any case, it is older than the portrait at the Royal Society in London, donated to England by Stanislas Augustus

## THE EDUCATION OF JAN SOBIESKI

The course of studies of Jan Sobieski, the future Polish King John III, is known chiefly from the work on this subject by

The background of the portrait of Copernicus' father, shows a figure of the Madonna, and a mountainous landscape with the ruins of a Gothic cathedral and round Renaissance temples symbolizing two epochs — the Middle Ages and the Renaissance. The great astronomer believed that the circular shape best expressed creative perfection. It cannot be excluded that the painting is by Copernicus himself, but this hypothesis can hardly be proved since the original no longer exists

This room adjoining the assembly hall contains mementos connected with Copernicus, such as instruments for the measurement of stars, an astrolabe, a turquetum, a celestial globe and portraits

Henryk Barycz (1938). Let us add that John III's granddaughter, Klementyna Sobieska married James Stuart, the young Pretender and last claimant to the throne of Scotland. In the year 1640, Jakub Sobieski, Voivode of Lublin, prepared a letter of instruction for the education of his two sons — Jan, aged 10, and his elder brother Marek. Jakub Sobieski himself was an alumnus of the University. The letter offers a good picture of the education of a young Polish nobleman in the 17th century.

The young Sobieskis arrived in Cracow in 1640 with a retinue of nine teachers and servants. They took up their residence in a separate house and, for the next five years, were educated at the Nowodworski school and at the University. Sons of other magnate families (the Sieniawskis, Koniecpolskis, Potockis, Ostrorógs) studied in the same way. Attention was mainly paid to a general education useful to a "statist" i.e. statesman or leader — in parliament, in war, or in the diplomatic service. Instruction included Latin and foreign languages (the latter were taught privately), rudiments of philosophy, somewhat less mathematics (approached from the point of view of its utility in artillery and land-surveying), natural sciences and geography. Much time was taken up by religion including daily services, membership in fraternities, vows, and sacraments. In competition with Jesuit schools and under the pressure of the anti-reformation bishops, the University established two fraternities: the Rosary Fraternity in 1621 and the Academic Sodality in 1631.

It was in secondary school that the young Sobieski learned most. His surviving copybooks for rhetoric, Polish stylistics, and other school papers show that his education encouraged civic virtues, emphasized the Turkish danger to the State, and encouraged attachment to the ruling dynasty, to the religion, and to Latin culture.

This education was not free of shortcomings. Already in secondary school, there was a division between the sons of rich noblemen and those of poor burghers and peasants. Although Jan's father, Voivode Sobieski, clearly expressed the desire that his sons should study with others, "not according to birth or titles" — there is

This portrait of John III by the Cracow artist Jan Trycjusz (1677), presents the King in nobleman's dress, i.e. a golden gown and fur-lined cape. Sobieski attended the Nowodworski School run by the University

ing language exercises in Latin, they did little to improve the pupils' minds. The future triumphant victor of Vienna never mastered Polish spelling and his writings are in the typically involved style of the period.

Sobieski remained attached to the University. On his way to the Vienna campaign against the Turks he visited the Collegium Maius and his former tutor, Wojciech Dąbrowski. After the campaign he offered to the University Persian rugs of rare beauty, taken from the enemy, which have in part been preserved to the present day.

## THE CONFLICT WITH THE JESUITS

It is not easy to form an opinion on the dispute between the University and the Jesuits because present-day historians of the conflict hold differing views on the matter. The Jesuits were the attacking side and represented educational cosmopolitism — though of a high standard —

The top of what is traditionally held to have been John III's camp table. It is decorated with sheet silver, representing the triumph of Mars and Venus — an allusion to the persons of the King and Marie Casimire

reason to doubt whether this actually was so.

In fact, the Nowodworski school was overcrowded. Cramped in the class-rooms were several dozen pupils who made notes on their knees. The richer youths were seated more comfortably, closer to the professor, and the poorer pupils farther away. It was only in the larger lectoria of the Collegium Maius that this division into rich and poor was obliterated.

In the Collegium Maius the future king attended Professor Speronowicz's lectures on Aristotelian philosophy, although they can have been of little value. Other lectures on ancient literature and the interpretation of Aristotle's "Politics" or of the works of Cicero, were also based on medieval scholasticism. Apart from offer-

John III, presented as a Roman victor on an Italian-made ivory bas-relief, surely dating from after 1683, the date of the Vienna victory

What interests us here mainly are the picturesque details of the conflict that lasted for two hundred years. To the deliberate and cunning provocations of the Jesuits, who had the support of the Kings Stephen Batory and Sigismund III, the University responded with printed pamphlets, which were often quite primitive, although even respectable scholars such as Jan Brożek did not hesitate to write them. These polemics are quite well known to us, because they have been carefully preserved in the Jagiellonian Library. The first was the anonymous pamhlet *Equitis Poloni in Jezuitos actio prima* (1590). It was followed by others, like *The Shield of Defence of the Professors of the Cracow Academy* (1623) and, above all *Gratis* by Jan Brożek. Whether the University did or did not in some

while the University was already at that time a provincial school, poor in original ideas and means but trying to provide an education to meet social needs. Aleksander Brückner, author of the *History of Polish Culture*, was convinced that the University had been wrong to oppose for two hundred years the transformation of Jesuit colleges into higher schools, since this would have improved the standards of education in Poland. Professor Henryk Barycz, on the other hand, wrote: "In spite of all the shortcomings and of the scarcely edifying methods employed in the conflict, the objectives of the University were right and far-sighted".

When they launched their offensive against the University's monopoly in higher education, the Jesuits were aware that the battle would not be an easy one. The Provincial of the Order wrote to his General in Rome in 1582: "The inauguration of the College in Cracow involves great dangers, because the University, which enjoys a high reputation in Poland although its actual standing is not so high, will be hostile to us and will instigate the whole country against us".

GRATIS.⁴¹
Abo
DISCVRS I.
Ziemiänina z Plebanem.
Ziemiänin, Pleban.

Anti-Jesuit dialogue from 1625, ascribed to Jan Brożek. A fragment of it reads: "Landowner: How then, can the capital city be at war? Vicar: Truly I know not how it began. I sent Matthew to Cracow... that he might study at the Grand Collegium; now he... tells me strange stories of Jesuits starting their own schools"

Apart from the dispute in print there were student disturbances. When a student called Przepiórka from Mazovia was killed, the University laid responsibility on the Jesuits. With minor changes, the controversy continued until the 18th century. It never entered anyone's mind that it was possible to reach a compromise which would have been beneficial to both sides.

Aleksander Brückner writes: "The Academy did not care too much for education, but rather for its own monopolistic position. Education would not have suffered, because in emulation a Jesuit academy did not care too much for educaheight of those in Ingolstadt or Graz, which still attracted so many Poles in the 17th century. In any case having exhausted its resources in this unjust cause, the University sank into a deep sleep from which Father Kołłątaj roused it only a century and a half later".

In the course of the centuries, after the dissolution of the Order, the controversy with the Jesuits was transformed into a struggle by the University for independence and even for survival .Here are the title pages of two pamphlets containing discussions between Cracow and Warsaw in 1789. The author of one was Andrzej Trzciński, professor of physics in Cracow, the other was written by Franciszek Siarczyński, a Warsaw author

way assist in the publication of Zachowski's world-famous *Monita secreta,* the apocryph which caused so much damage to the Jesuit Order, it is hard to say. (The first edition of 1615 was probably printed in Poland).

The Jesuits of course hit back and also responded with pamphlets. They found out that the Brożek pamphlet had been printed by a dissenter and the man was punished.

We have already noted that in our opinion more was involved in the struggle against the Jesuits than the local ambitions of the University. What was at stake was the independence of Polish Catholicism from Rome, and Poland's national identity, which was bound up neither with the East nor with her Western neighbours, but rather with Italy, not however, in subservience, but in active collaboration.

## DISPUTES

Professor had their altercations, not only over scientific matters but often over wordly incomes and honours.

These disputes, which recur again and again in the Rector's records, involved slander, invective and even fights especially in earlier times when manners were rougher. However, as most of these rows occurred in the Collegium Minus, where junior professors lived, we feel absolved from dealing with them in this description of the Collegium Maius, which lodged elder and more dignified scholars. There existed the custom which is frequently mentioned in the records of the Rector's courts — of nailing pamphlets, lampoons or controversial theses to the doors of the Collegium Maius. It was an old custom, widespread all over Europe in the days when newspapers were not yet known. In 1526, the English poet Leonard Coxe nailed to the door of the Collegium poems against Erasm Jan Empedophilus — for which he was later brought to trial before the Rector. A hundred years later, the printer Franciszek Cezary the younger also nailed a declaration to the door of the Collegium for which he too was brought up before the Rector's court.

Several noteworthy rows took place in Collegium Maius, too. In 1563, Michał from Wiślica flew into such a passion at a meeting in the Common Room that he tilted over a heavy table on his adversaries and had to pay for the damage done. In 1558, Master Wojciech Wędrochowski was compelled to ask forgiveness of Jan Leopolita for having threatened him. The same Wędrochowski broke into the library in the Collegium Maius and took away various books. Professor Joachim Sperenowicz became an exasperating troublemaker and picker of quarrels in his old age (in 1653 he broke his walking-stick over Professor S. Wieczorkiewicz). In 1692, Professor Wojciech Krzykawski forfeited his academic rights for insulting the Cracow's municipal authorities in a sermon delivered in St. Mary's Church. In 1662, disturbances broke out among professors over a marble plaque with an inscription commemorating the University's royal benefactors, which was placed in the Collegium Maius by Professor Marcin Radymiński. The dispute was started by Andrzej Kucharski, an ambitious and digruntled member of the College, and by the equally troublesome Professor Marcin Solikowski.

At the beginning of the 17th century, a great deal of trouble was caused to the University by Professor Wojciech Sierpiec, a member of the Collegium Maius, who for several decades owned the village of Sidzina near Tyniec. He was a ruthless master and maltreated his peasants physically and morally. When we read the relevant archive accounts (discovered by Professor H. Barycz), we cannot help wondering why it did not occur to anyone at the time that Sierpiec was simply insane. Scandals involving him, citations, complaints, and punishments, dragged on for twenty years in the Rector's courts, showing that the University authorities lacked energy and resolution.

The scholarly dispute in 1561 between Julian Górski and Benedykt Herbest over a minor problem of grammar, was rather than otherwise amusing and would have been even more so if Herbest had not left the University as a result. There were also unsavoury mutual denunciations and accusations (Krzysztof Najmanowicz against Sebastian Petrycy in 1615, M. Solikowski against M. Radymiński over the latter's alleged collaboration with the Swedes, etc.).

Among the less serious offences was the case of Master Marcin Korzeniowski in 1615. Under the influence of drink his closest friend, Professor Zachariasz Starnigiel, showered abuse on him at a party in the house of the Cracow councilman Frąckiewicz. The case was brought before the Rector.

In the 1760's, the University was involved

in a quarrel with Bishop Kajetan Sołtyk over roofs and a lease in the village of Luborzyca. Sołtyk went to the length of beating up the leaseholders of an inn. When he finally lost the case (after appealing as high as Rome), he suddenly veered round and made his peace with the University.

Kołłątaj relates: "The bishop especially came to Cracow and put up at the palace in Prądnik. The ceremonial of the formal apology was carefully planned. Sołtyk sent his carriages for the University seniors and invited them to dinner. The academicians brought with them all the other professors and students. Abundant drink and a splendid banquet, not only for the seniors but even for the students, set matters right again".

In the 18th century, Professor Jan Polaczek became the victim of much, ill will. He occupied a modest groundfloor apartment in Collegium Maius (on the Jagiellońska Street side) and led a life considered queer, quite different from that of his colleagues. He preferred church fairs, peasant gathering, to the company of the rich and the learned. Nor was he averse to drink. His colleagues eventually forced him to resign his chair, which he accepted with equanimity. Kołłątaj's account of this story reveals his sympathy for Polaczek and criticism of the intolerant academicians of Cracow.

In 1787, during Stanislas Augustus' visit to Cracow, Józef Bogucicki, professor of ecclesiastical history, came out with a eulogy of religious freedom in a lecture on the history of Hussitism. He immediately became the object of attacks by fanatical theologians, and Primate Poniatowski himself had to use his authority to shield him.

In 1787, during Stanislas Augustus' visit sity, there was a renowned quarrel between Professor Andrzej Trzciński, Chairman of the College of Physics, and his colleagues, who refused to accept the fact that he had been made dean not by election but by appointment by the Commission of National Education. Moreover he was also accused of ignorance. The campaign against him was led by Śniadecki. Trzciński sued Professors Scheidt and Radwański, while the College sued Trzciński and entered a complaint in the municipal records. The case was eventually won by Śniadecki, who did not however, succeed in removing Trzciński from his chair.

These old quarrels should not perhaps be judged by today's standards. Customs were different then, and those describing the disputes were not always objective. At any rate, in the last quarter of the 19th century the University entered upon a period of peaceful development.


## THE RECTOR'S JURISDICTION

The Rector's judicial powers were exerted from the very outset to moderate the quarrelsomeness of youth. Ladislas Jagiełło's Charter of 1400 says: "(...) The Rector shall pass judgment on students who commit minor offences such as tearing out hair, hitting with hand or fist so that blood is drawn, or any violence of not too serious a nature". On the whole, the Rector was neither very resolute nor severe. For most excesses, such as fights, brawls in town, or love affairs, the delinquents were usually confined to a dark cell which has survived in the Collegium Maius to the present day.

At the beginning of the 15th century, Stanisław of Skalbmierz recalled in his rector's speech the eternal sins of the students. "They are lazy," the Rector reproved them, "they do not pay tuition or other fees, all they think of are clothes or banquets or their mistress's bed. Nor do they show due respect to the professors".

Complaints and even thunderous attacks on professors for their faults and sins were also a stock item of the rector's speeches.

Strict rules and interdictions were intended to safeguard the morals of the University community. Inns where wine and beer were served were off limits for both masters and students. They were not allowed, either, to amuse themselves in the company of women, strolling players or vagrants.

Yet life was stronger than bans; and inns and other entertainments never lacked customers. The Rector's courts also heard complaints against dormitory seniors who had to explain debts, scandals or love affairs.

Entrance to the dark cell where students were confined by Rector's verdict. The punished students often managed to escape with outside assistance, by breaking the door open or filing off the lock

Here is a typical Rector's verdict dating from 18th century: "Whereas the students, in disregard of their vocation, had the audacity to change their clothes and move about armed both in the daytime and at night, to play musical instruments at night, to roam the squares and streets, and to attack, maul and wound on a public road i.e. in Grodzka Street, the attendants of the lady wife of the Castellan of Sandomierz, therefore His Magnificence the Rector, by way of punishment, ordered them to be detained in the dark cell for a whole week during lectures in decent clothes sparing them, however, expulsion from the University, which they richly deserve for such excesses."

The behaviour of the youth was difficult to control and caused the educators much trouble. Students were often inclined to pranks and rows and even more serious offences. There were frequent practical jokes and outbursts of rowdyness connected with the initiation of freshmen (the so-called *beaniae*). In ceremony known as the "Drowning of Judas" an effigy of Judas, dressed in rags, was dragged about town amidst all kinds of pranks aimed especially against dissenters. The effigy was eventually thrown down from the tower of St. Mary's Church and to the yelling of the mob it was burned in public, and the ashes scattered. There was plenty of time for such amusements because while vacations were unknown, frequent feast days were observed and every opportunity was taken to secure a short break in studies.

The *beaniae,* or custom of harrassing new students until they had ransomed themselves once or even twice, was known in Cracow but disappeared in the 16th century. Moreover it was never so popular as in Germany and Bohemia where it was also observed more frequently in craft guilds.

It should be noted that such customs as going from house to house "with a mug", singing and tumbling the election of a student king, etc. — which are today favourite themes for columnists and stage-directors — were often cultivated by school pupils, rather than by university students. The latter were less frivolous, especially in the 15th century, if only because they were hedged about much more dormitory and college regulations. In the 16th and 17th century, increasing rowdyness became a serious problem for which the chief blame must fall on the University. Until the first half of the 16th century the Rector's courts prevented offences, but later on — and especially in the 17th century — students misbehaved with growing impunity.

The students' rebellion, rendered famous by Matejko and in literature marks a turning point between medieval discipline and later laxity. In 1549, the pupils of Cracow schools staged demonstrations in connection with the killing of a pupil in All Saints' Dormitory. They accused a priest called Czarnkowski of murder (without grounds) and when they failed to obtain the satisfaction they demanded either from the king or from the authorities, they declared they would leave Cracow which they did in fact, not succeed in doing. To blame for the whole affair was Bishop Samuel Maciejowski, who behaved far too passively towards those who had actually committed the murder.

The University, on the one hand, insisted on a monastic system of education and on an anachronistic system of jurisdiction; on the other hand, the educators themselves, and in particular the dormitory seniors, assistants and tutors, as well as elder professors, often failed to set an edifying example. In the 17th century, the medieval laws were no longer adequate and sufficient for the developing society.

Added to all this was religious fanaticism. The youth were incited against dissenters or excesses against the latter were overlooked, since they had the appearance of religious devotion. These student disturbances were far from funny: they included brawls among students going from house to house to get a meal; the destruction of the Protestant church called "Bróg" in Jana Street (in 1574); a raid on a butchers' house in 1597; the gang of student who attacked Chorowice; scuffles with city guards in the "Salamander

This drawing from 1574 presents the hardly creditable exploit of the University students, namely the demolition of a Protestant chapel in St. John Street. The caption reads:
"This was how the Cracow Church was pulled down.
If you were busy and did not see it done,
Then look, brother, how with axes the door they chop,
While others wrestle with the gratings on top"

House" in 1660 (with casualties in killed and wounded) and in the "Grey House" in 1682 ; the extortion of money at the dissenters' funeral (1683). In 1753, riots broke out against the city guards known as "herrings". Students, together with young artisans got control of the city and arsenal, and even threatened the municipal authorities.

Here for instance is an example of a somewhat riotous student : "Szymon Twardowski, brother of the poet who wrote Polish poems *ex tempore,* son of a burgher from Sambor, studied in the Academy anno 1625 and, since he prowled in town by night, he was expelled. He wounded one Jastrzębski servant to the Castellan of Cracow, Prince of Zbaraż — and for this latter excess he just barely managed to save his throat by fleeing the city".

The charges that the Rector's rule was too lenient, are well founded. It would have been better if the Rector's jurisdiction had been limited to offences committed on University grounds.

On the other hand, however, the University protected the students. This was experienced by young Pląszkowski who was behind time in paying the enrolment fee and, when he was beaten, had no one to stand up for him : "Jakub Pląszkowski from Węgrowiec in Great-Poland, son of a town tailor, came to Cracow anno 1637. He was about 24 years old and dressed like a seminarist. Indeed he was a student but did not learn, and when one day some burghers' sons beat him up, and the Academy did nothing about it, only then did he comply with the requirements of enrolment".

## WITCHCRAFT PRACTICES

Legends and rumours about witchcraft practices, alchemy and cabals have been persistently associated with the Collegium Maius building. From the middle of the 15th century, the occult sciences gained ground rapidly in Cracow, not only in the University but also outside it, in monasteries and at the royal court. Rector's courts at that time more than once held witchtrials. In the 16th century, some professors (e.g. Walenty Fontana) openly attacked quack doctors.

According to certain foreign sources (German and English), the famous sorcerer, Doctor Faustus, is supposed to have studied in Cracow. *The Life and Adventures of Doctor Faust,* published in Frankfort-on-Main in 1587, says that Faust travelled to Cracow, Poland, to the then famous University and found himself there in the company of kindred spirits who used "Chaldean, Persian, Arabic and Greek words, figures, letters, incantations, spells and names, and whatever names, oaths and charms anyone might wish". Alanius, a disciple of Melanchthon, wrote in 1590 : "Faust esset scholasticus cracoviensis". The English *Ballad of the Life and Death of Faust* (1587) mentions Cracow as the place where he studied. At the same time, the story of Twardowski's sorcery told by Łukasz Górnicki in the Courtier dates from the same time. The fact that the Jagiellonian University attracted learned cabbalists from abroad is shown by the visit to Cracow of the English alchemist and astronomer John Dee. In 1584, he visited the library in the Collegium Maius and made a present of Boethius' book *De consolatione philosophiae* with the following inscription in beautiful handwriting : "In order to adorn with one more very rare work the illustrious library of the Cracow University which has already been splendidly endowed with books from all fields of science and learning, having in view both the benefit that will result thereof in the future to the commonwealth of letters, and the desire to manifest by this modest gift my friendliness towards the Honourable Marian Glicjusz, a most distinguished scholar and sagacious man, the worthiest Rector of this University, and towards the other best professors and scholars, and as a token of my readiness to render services — I, John Dee, of England, expert in Christian philosophy and mathematical sciences, offer this very ancient book to this library, to be forever used by scholars, and I dedicate it with my own hand with the greatest pleasure and devotion. 24 November, the year of Our Lord 1584, John Dee, of London".

From the 17th century, rumours multiplied concerning a mysterious book of magic in the possession of the University. It was said that the book known as *Liber Magnus* had been borrowed and taken to

Vilna by Sigismund Augustus when he dabbled in magic. According to an account by A. Naramowski from 1724, the Jesuit D. Butwił, experienced a true onslaught of evil spirits when he read the book. In the middle of the 17th century, the book found its way to the Collegium Iuridicum (*Cracoviae est liber a quodam monacho manuscriptus distante diabolo* — 1640), and later-on to the Collegium Maius, where it was said to have been

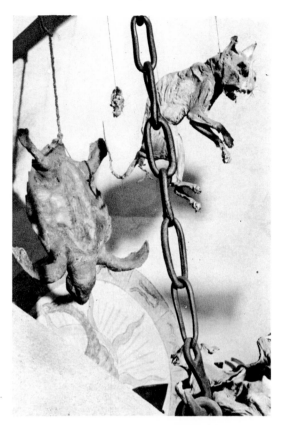

Magic powers were also ascribed to animals. In the walls of the Collegium, cats were immured alive at one time to protect the inhabitants against evil. The mummified bodies of the poor creatures are preserved today among other mementos of former black magic practices

The imprint of a "devil paw" by the old lock. Magic signs of this kind were intended as protection against thieves or other mischief

buried under Radymiński's marble plaque (which was obviously impossible). The "Liber Magnus" is now in the Jagiellonian Library and turns out to have nothing to do with magic, but to be a scientific chiefly medical, encyclopaedia, written in the middle of the 15th century by the Czech scholar Paul Zitek from Prague. The ostensible imprint of a devil's paw in the book is in reality a blot of spilled ink.

Archeological and historical research conducted on the premise of Collegium Maius corroborates the rumours that black magic and maybe even witchcraft was practised within its walls. In 1951 the body of a cat was found under the vault of the Libraria (constructed in 1516); the animal must have been buried alive under rubble as an offering to keep off evil. This is not the only trace of this kind of

Old flasks in which liquids were mixed in the search for chemical and alchemic formulae

16th c. Cracow woodcut showing an armillary sphere together with two learned astronomers engaged in a dispute

sad superstition in Cracow. Human beings were also sacrificed for the same purpose; as is shown by the human skeletons discovered in 1913 in the vaults over rooms in the West wing of the Wawel Castle. Let us recall that the physician Karl Widman from Augsburg dedicated to Sigismund III his work *Secreta Secretorum*, which explained how drugs and magic potions could be extracted from human and animal mummies. The above-

15th-century Venetian goblet with the coat of arms of King Alexander or King Olbracht (c. 1500). Glasses of this kind were used in magic ceremonies

mentioned mummy of a cat is evidence of the same superstitions and belief in witchcraft among masons. Practices of this kind in the Collegium were the source of legends that later grew around this building.

As further research is undertaken, evidence of magic practices in the Collegium multiply. Bricks with imprints of dog's paws have been found everywhere in the walls, and this again is not accidental. Even today such a paw mark on a brick is believed to be the trace of the devil's hand, just like the black spot in the Paulus Encyclopaedia in Prague. Since the dog is an animal that guards man's prop-

94

"We are both the same" — a woodcut used by Cracow printers shows the symbolical figures of Medicine and Astrology. It was commonly believed that man's health depends on the course of the stars and constellations

erty and thus repels evil, it was believed that the trace of a dog's paw also performed this task.

As has already been mentioned, information on Dr. Faustus's stay in Cracow and his studies at the Jagiellonian University was better known abroad than in Poland. In 1790, Goethe accompanied the Prince of Weimar on his travels to Cracow from Silesia. His guide in Cracow was Professor Franciszek Scheidt, and it is quite likely that he was interested in the Collegium Maius. After all, that was the place where the hero of the great poet's masterpiece was supposed to have studied.

Magic, alchemy, astrology, superstitions and the objects connected with them, the years of Faust's studies in Cracow, the story of Master Twardowski — all this still awaits historical investigation. It is difficult to establish the role played in all these matters by the Collegium Maius and by its collections of curiosities which were surrounded by an aura of sensation but which in reality were the germ of later scientific collections. At any rate, some of the discoveries made in the course of the latest restoration of the Collegium Maius, confirms the fact that Cracow legends connected with our building contain a good deal of truth as far as unions superstitions are concerned.

A reconstruction of an alchemist's stove in the "Alchemy" room. Assembled in this corner are natural and other curiosities from the University collections

## ST. ANNE'S CHURCH

The picture of University customs would not be complete if we did not mention the important role played by the Church of St. Anne's across the street from the Collegium Maius. It is one of Poland's most interesting churches and testifies to the good taste and architectural know-how of the professors who financed and personally directed its construction.

The University patronage is of old standing. St. Anne's Church was founded in the 14th century and in 1418, Jagiełło bestowed upon the University tutors and the abbot of Mogiła the church patronage. It was endowed with incomes which helped to support junior professors of philosophy and pensioners. In the 16th century (1535), it was elevated to the rank of collegiate church.

St. Anne's Church became the centre of various university ceremonies and meetings chief among them being religious services. It was also the place where disputations took place, degrees were conferred and welcoming held. Funerals also played an important role. Distinguished professors were laid to rest in the vaults of the church. The pride of the University was Professor Jan Wacięga of Kęty. whose cult grew in the 17th century and who was canonized in 1767, which strengthened the position of the University in relation to Jesuit schools. On the other hand, it brought about a reaction later (in Kołłątaj's time) because the cult of Saint John turned the University away from secular education.

The present Church of St. Anne is the third successive church to stand on this site. It was built in the years 1689—1703 at a cost of half a million zlotys. The architect Tylman of Gameren, the sculptor Baltazar Fontana, who came from Moravia, the painter Karol Dankwart from Nysa and Innocent Monti from Moravia, decorated the church in the late Roman baroque style in accordance with the wishes of the professors who directed the construction work and are primarily responsible for its appearance. The University's links with Rome and Roman architecture and the expert knowledge of Professors Sebastian Piskorski and An-

drzej Buchowski were characteristic of Cracow at a time when French art prevailed in Warsaw.

The wealth of traditions, dignity, predilection for ornateness, and emphasis on ceremonies hid from sight many a hole in the professors' gowns, it is true, but they also helped the university to survive many a difficult moment. They were an expression of something more than personal vanity and an inclination to pomp. This failed to be properly understood for a long time, and even today is sometimes misinterpreted by those who either underestimate or fear the role of imagination and feeling. How very often voices depreciating baroque art are raised among our clergy, and how much damage this superb style suffers in our churches

The Church of St. Anne, built at the turn of the 17th and 18th centuries, served the University not only for religious purposes but also for academic ceremonies. The interior is perhaps Poland's best example of baroque

because of this! To return to St. Anne's Church, it should be emphasized that its dependence on the Italian baroque (although the artists who decorated it were brought to Cracow from Moravia), was connected in the 17th century with the belief that the University, like the whole country should look South for its culture.

## TEMPORARY RECESS

Among the lesser known periods in the University's history are the years after the third partition of Poland, when the University remained alone, with no protectors, persecuted and doomed to closure (after 1805). And yet, even then, some professors (whose names we unfortunately do not know), summoned up enough courage to take part in the secret Republicans' Society, to act in support of Kołłątaj who was imprisoned in Olmütz, to maintain contacts with Kościuszko and with the republican government of France — all this in spite of the fact that the situation at the University was becoming more and more difficult, or even downright hopeless.

Towards the end of the 18th century, all traditions and customs seemed doomed. The Kołłątaj reform had treated them mercilessly for in the eagerness to build a new and better school, whatever was old was scrapped. The Kościuszko Insurrection, the third partition and the subsequent years of Austrian rule (up to 1809) reinforced these losses.

The furnishings of the halls, lectoria and professors' lodgings were sold by auction or dissipated and if the library under the management of Jacek Przybylski, survived, it was mainly because hardly anyone took interest in it (although the Austrians intended to take it to Vienna). Needless to say, many valuable curios were removed from the library, on the alleged grounds of having little to do with science.

Not only the Austrian authorities were responsible for these depradations. The value of old relics was quite often ignored by Poles themselves. In the first years of the 19th century, Cracow was impoverished by the demolition of old walls, churches and of the city hall. Shortly af-

St. Anne's Church has long been linked with the University. A view from the Plantations clearly shows its noble proportions, its lofty dome and the two-towered façade. Painting by Saturnin Świerzyński (1863)

ter the incorporation of Cracow into the Duchy of Warsaw, the nonsensical decision was taken to transfer the University archives to Warsaw. It was not until a few years later that they were recovered.

This is how Jan Śniadecki criticized the abolition of University traditions:

"University life — modest and absorbed in learning alone, the simple, godly and honest customs, the ancient dignity of the corps, the splendour of academic ceremonies, the fame of the nation's first school acquired in the past, although constantly harmed by the slanders of the envious Order, — all this attracted youth to the University.

"Under the reform, these sacred and beneficial institutions should have been upheld and preserved, should have been restored by a better selection and plan of learning, by providing all necessary equipment for studies; the opportunity should have been taken to establish with due deliberation grades and prizes in each discipline to raise the importance of academic degrees and titles, to offer rewards through remunerative service in so many Voivodship schools — and, then perhaps

The memory of these two men is revered in the University with deepest gratitude. The astronomer Jan Śniadecki was not only an illustrious professor but a steadfast champion of the University's rights in the difficult years after the First Partition of Poland. Hugo Kołłątaj was a great reformer of the University who, from 1778, set it on a new road of development. Śniadecki's portraits is by Alfred Remer (c. 1885) and Kołłątaj's by Jan Pffeiffer (c. 1812)

the Cracow Academy would have become, with lesser expenditure of effort and means, a model educational institution, organized to the advantage of learning and of the country. An altogether opposite way of reform was chosen. The academic ceremonies, judged pedantic, were relinquished, the former commencements were abolished, the list of academicians was confined to salaried candidates, old and distinguished men were dismissed, thus encouraging the young to make little account of merit and former importance; the salaries of all teachers were equalized as though everyone's difficulties and pains in learning, talents, abilities and assiduity were equal and did not call for further encouragement. Within the space of one year, impressions that had been developed and imparted to others, in the course of centuries were obliterated and it was never possible to renew or revive them again."

Let us not regret, however, that the medieval structure of the college disappeared. The changes which we call "the Kołłątaj reform" were indeed a necessity and a result of "new time". Certain English Universities did not undergo such reforms and have retained the old system; today they are reproached — not without reason — with excessive traditionalism.

Hard times were coming to the Jagiellonian University. If it survived them, it was due to the people educated in the period of the Kołłątaj reform.

No one perhaps gave a better characterization of the scientific life and old customs in the University than Kołłątaj himself in his description of the state of education in Poland in the 18th century: "Although the Cracow Academy was in poor condition as far as education and knowledge were concerned, it was none the less an ancient institution, not inferior in many achievements to Europe's most famous academies".

The professors who remembered old University customs either retired or left Cracow, as did Jan Śniadecki. In 1803, at the time of Austrian rule, he wrote to Kołłątaj:

"I watched in Cracow the overthrow of all good reforms introduced in the Academy by the Commission of Education. I turned my eyes away from so sad a sight and finally resolved to devote myself to a quiet and private life and to sever all my ties with the Academy since I could not be useful to it any longer in any way."

Rector Sebastian Sierakowski tried to revive the University traditions when in 1821 (in the "Free City" period) he renovated the Jagiellonian Room and commissioned the artist Michał Stachowicz to paint scenes from the history of the University. This frieze has not survived and is known from copies only. Its naïveté exerts a peculiar charm and helped to arouse respect for the traditions and customs of the University.

## THE 19TH CENTURY

The history of the University in the 19th century may be divided into two periods. The first period — until 1870 (i.e. the years of the Free City and the subsequent period of the Austrian occupation was characterized by restraint, vexation and constant changes; the second period of autonomy under Austrian rule saw the sudden revival of the Polish spirit of the University and its vital and rapid growth. The first period, in spite of the appearance of independence, was marked by incessant pressure exerted by political patrons (in particular by the Austrian Minister Metternich) who saw in the University a hotbed of liberal and even revolutionary tendencies. The University waged for years a struggle for the freedom of teaching and, as a rule, suffered defeat. It managed, however, to prolong its existence. Had it not been for the system of autonomy which the Habsburg Monarchy was compelled to adopt, one may doubt whether the University would have survived the 19th century.

Yet it not only survived but flourished. In all faculties, but especially in those of law, philosophy and medicine, Polish scholars finally came into prominence and, from 1869, Polish became the language of instruction. As late as the 1860's, the Ministry in Vienna endeavoured to maintain centralism but its interference was soon limited to administrative matters. In 1873, the Academy of Learning was established in Cracow, having grown out of the Cracow Learned Society.

Although the development of research and teaching was by no means easy, the University, from the beginning of the 19th century, paid special attention to history. It all began with the activities of such professors as Józef Sołtykowicz, Jerzy Samuel Bandtkie, Józef Muczkowski, and of other scholars working outside the University but remaining under its influence (Ambroży Grabowski, Jurzyński,

Karol Estreicher Sr., director of the Jagiellonian Library, bibliographer and drama historian (1827—1908) as portrayed by Leon Wyczółkowski in the Cracow theatre at the first night of Wyspiański's "Wedding"

The Collegium Novum — the imposing University building, erected in the years 1883—1887 to a design by F. Księżarski

The Assembly Hall in the Collegium Novum

Feliks Bentkowski). In the next two generations, Cracow became the capital of the historical sciences in Poland.

We are not concerned here with the history of the University in the 19th century, however, but with the history of customs and events as seen against the background of the Collegium Maius. It can be generally stated that until 1840 university life in Cracow was characterized by the justifiably prudent attitude of the University authorities. The partitioning Powers entrusted the administration of the University to a body bombastically named the Grand Council which was a numerous assembly of dignitaries having little in common with learning or teaching. The Rector, Deans and Senate were helpless, all the more so that the Free City's Commissioner of Education interfered even in such trivialities as the sweeping of chimneys and other domestic matters in the Collegium Maius. While Universities abroad acquired new buildings, received grants, inaugurated new chairs and departments, the Jagiellonian University was subjected to such mortifications that it seems almost unbelievable that it succeeded in surviving the attacks of the spiteful bureaucracy. In spite of all these difficulties, life in the Collegium Maius was gradually revitalised in the first half of the 19th century, due to the energy and knowledge of two directors of the library — Jerzy Samuel Bandtkie and Józef Muczkowski. As soon as the Library obtained new rooms on the 1st floor, these two distinguished specialists in literature, bibliography, palaeography and other historical sciences, were able to add to its possessions, make up a catalogue and open the Library to the public.

The structure of the University, created in the second half of the 19th century, has survived until the present day. Beside the faculties, an ever greater role has been played in the University by the various institutes which act as research centres and have gradually turned into separate institutions. This seems to be the most essential change and is a process that is not yet completed. As a result of specialization and the setting up of new chairs, the importance of the faculties (departments) is gradually decreasing while that of separate studies and institutes is constantly growing. They often perform inter-departmental and even inter-university functions.

In 1863—64, the critical year of the January Rising, the enrolment amounted to 371 students, including 66 in the faculty of theology, 129 in law, 88 in medicine and 46 in "philosophy" (the humanities and natural sciences). Pharmaceutics constituted a separate department with an enrolment of 12.

That period saw the restoration of old University customs. It has already been mentioned that on the occasion of the Austrian Emperor's visit in 1851, Rector Majer and the members of the University Senate donned gowns again as they did not want to appear in uniforms. A little later, chains and maces for the various faculties were acquired.

## ELECTIONS OF ACADEMIC AUTHORITIES

Since the introduction of the so-called University autonomy, the Rector and Deans have been elected by their colleagues. In the old days, elections were held once a year because such was the duration of the term of office. This had certain advantages, for the professors were not overburdened by administrative duties; it also prevented the formation in the University of a ruling clique. But it had its drawbacks, because it disrupted the continuity of work and the administration of the University was turned over to secretaries of the Rector's office and of the faculties. In the period between World War I, and World War II, a two-year term of office for the Rector was introduced; after World War II this was changed to a three-year term.

The elections were held in spring, in the Stuba Communis in the Collegium Maius. The electors took seats at tables and the nomination of candidates began. If there was no unanimity, then, as a rule, only positive opinions on the various candidates were voiced. From the tone of those opinions, it could be inferred who was best fitted for the Rector's post.

The ceremony of handing over authority to the new Rector by his predecessor is combined with the inauguration of the academic years in the beginning of October. Professors wearing gowns assemble in the Collegium Maius and form a long procession which passes through the whole Collegium, i.e. the Assembly Hall, library and common room. In the Assembly Hall beadles dip the maces before the portraits of patrons, benefactors and professors. The whole procession then proceeds along St. Anne's Street and the Plantations to the Collegium Novum. Every year, a crowd of spectators watch and applaud the procession and take pictures with unflagging interest.

The proper inauguration ceremony of the new school year takes place in the Assembly Hall of the Collegium Novum.

If it coincides with a new Rector's term, then the transference of authority to the new Rector takes place after the outgoing Rector has made his report. The new incumbent is first handed the grand mace, a gift of Cardinal Frederick Jagiellon, inscribed with the Latin words: *Accipe sceptrum regiminis*. He places the mace on the desk in front of him and then the outgoing Rector takes off the Rector's chain and hands it to his successor with the words: *Accipe catenam dignitatis*. The new Rector puts on the chain and finally, the outgoing Rector takes off his finger the big, heavy ring, a gift of the province of Greater Poland from 1900, and puts it on the new Rector's finger, saying: *Accipe annulum sponsialem*. Now the new Rector makes a speech which he concludes with the words: *Quod Felix, Faustum, Fortunatumque Sit* — May the new year be a happy, propicious and fortunate one. The ceremony ends with the students' choir singing the old song *Gaude Mater Polonia!*.

## HIGHER DEGREES

The special ceremonies at which higher degrees were conferred, were abolished during the partition of Poland, but revived in the middle of the 19th century. In accordance with ancient custom, the Rector, Dean and Pro-Rector in gowns take their seats on the dais in the Assembly Hall, which is filled with guests and friends of the new doctor, the latter is then ushered into the Hall by two beadles carrying maces, who bow to the "pro-

Decisions of vital importance to the University are taken after exhaustive discussions of the academic Senate which often last long into the night

motors" (those conferring the degree) and dip their maces. Then the Promotor reads the Latin formula as it appears in the *Liber Iuramentorum Doctorandorum,* worded somewhat differently for each faculty. According to tradition, the formula was drawn up after medieval models by Józef Muczkowski the Elder, around 1850, and was subsequently modified several times. It opens with an invocation to the new doctor and the statement that he has submitted a thesis (the title of which is cited) and has defended it publicly in accordance with the relevant regulations.

The Promotor then recalls the duties of a doctor and calls upon him to take the oath. This is the Latin text :

Promotor : Doctorante Clarissime ! Dis-

The urn into which ballots are cast by members of the academic Senate during the voting

sertatione sub tituli ... conscripta et publice defensa atque examinibus summa cum lauda superatis quae lege constituta sunt ad explorandam doctrinam, eorum, qui doctoris nomen ac honores consequi student, adiisti nos, ut te eo honore appetiisti, in hoc solem ni consenssu ornaremus.

new docents are ceremoniously announced in the Assembly Hall of the Collegium Maius. Often the university grants honorary degrees to distinguished scholars or to eminent foreigners whom the Government may be interested in honouring.

The traditon of commencement ceremonies dates back to the Middle Ages. Academic degrees were once conferred in churches or monastery cloisters, but nowadays this ceremony is performed in University assembly halls. The place of honour in the hall is always occupied by the desk at which the Rector sits, with Pro-rectors and Deans at his sides. After handing over the diploma, the Rector congratulates the new doctor

petiisti, in hoc solem ni consenssu ornaremus. Haec to ex animi tui sententia spondebis ac pollicebere ?

Candidate : Spondeo ac polliceor.

Promotor : Ergo ego promotor legitime constituti munus te dominus N. N. ex decreto ordinis mei doctorem creo, creatum renuntio, omnia quae doctoris iura ac privilegia in te confero, in eiusque rei fidem hoc diploma, Universitatis sigillo insignitum, tibi in manus trado".

After the doctor has taken the oath, the promotors congratulate him and his friends and colleagues offer him gifts, usually flowers.

The formula of the oath is not just a picturesque custom. Unethical behaviour may cause the doctor to be struck off the University register. The "habilitation" or conferment of the title of ,,docent" in principle takes place only in those faculties where the docent obtains the so-called *Veniam Legendi* (which has to be approved by the supreme State authorities). Lately, however, the appointments of

At solemn academic occasions, professors of other universities appear in the gowns and caps of their schools. Here are representatives of Cambridge and Rome Universities during the Jagiellonian University's 600th anniversary celebrations

# YOUTH ORGANIZATIONS

The subject of this chapter does not converge with the history of the Collegium Maius until the 19th century, for at this time the Collegium housed the University library, where large numbers of students came to work. From the beginning of the 19th century, youth organizations played an ever greater role in University life.

In the Middle Ages, unions of students from the same country or territory, or of the same profession, were founded within a common dormitory or hostel. In the 15th century, Cracow had its Hungarian and German dormitories and Długosz founded a dormitory for students of law. There were always disputes and even disturbances among the students due to the fact that they came from different parts of the country. Lithuanians, Mazovians, Silesians, and students from Greater Poland, quarrelled with each other and with youth from Cracow. This encouraged the formation of unions or fraternities of which we know little, and which were presumably of a regional character.

At the beginning of the 17th century, the University began to set up religious fraternities after the Jesuit fashion, although all too often these sodalities and fraternities bred religious intolerance and initiated brawls against dissidents.

A charitable institution serving all the youth of Cracow was the students' hospital in Szpitalna Street. The hospital building has survived to our days and now houses theatrical collections. In time, the hospital was turned over to the parish of St. Mary's. Kołłątaj tried in vain to regain it for the University in 1778.

The first political youth organization was formed in 1655—1657 at the time of the Swedish "deluge". Its purpose was to oppose the Swedish invaders and to help the cause of John-Casimir. The membership included students, school pupils and young artisans. This conspiratorial organization had a military structure, a secret arsenal of weapons in the Carmelite Church and its own flag.

In the 18th century, we do not hear of any youth organizations, with an independent programme but at the very beginning of the 19th century a literary Friendship Circle was formed which aimed at self-education, especially in the field of literature.

At the time of the Napoleonic wars there must surely have been secret unions in Cracow too, but we know little about them. In 1820, students set up the White Eagle, but the Rector refused to allow it for fear of offending the Austrian authorities. In 1821, the Polish "Burschen" Fraternity was organized, on the lines of the Wrocław model. Its aim was to arouse enthusiasm and patriotic feelings through entertainments, excursions, singing, etc. It resembled the associations of Philomats and Philarets in Vilna. The organization was banned and there were arrests and investigations, for the occupying authorities feared youth organizations (and, so frequently did the Poles themselves).

The old traditions of outbreaks of rowdyness dating from the 17th and 18th centuries were still alive, but their character was different now for they were motivated by patriotic or social fervour. Among the most renowned demonstrations were those directed against the head of police, Antoni Kostecki, in 1820.

In the early 19th century, the custom developed in Cracow of excursions of school or University students accompanied by their teachers, known as May junkets. The destination was most frequently the nearby Bielany or Wolski Forest. These excursions were also attended by University professors, parents with daughters, as well as tutors. While Cracow was deserted at Bielany, games and amusements were in full swing.

At the time of the November Uprising (1830—31), there was student unrest, and meetings were held to expose the most oppressive and servile dignitaries. The hated Superintendent of Schools, General Załuski was forced to flee the city, and the President of the Senate of the Free City, Count Stanisław Wodzicki, had to resign. The movement, however, was not aimed against the University or the professors. The Rector was offered a ring with enamelled patriotic emblems as a token of appreciation for the help he showed to students joining the insurgent army.

In the years 1831—1850, emissaries from Polish emigrés abroad often visited Cracow. Bodies working for independence, such as the Philarets' Club (1832), the

Academic Association (1834), the Society of Rights (1835) and the Polish People's Association (1835), were revived under various names borrowed from emigré organizations. Among their most outstanding leaders were the historian of literature Lesław Łukaszewicz and the poet Gustaw Erenberg.

The Association for Mutual Education, formed in 1848, was a legal organization enjoying great popularity among students. Its members engaged in civic work, held scientific sessions and gave lectures in provincial towns (e.g. in Rzeszów). The Austrian authorities prohibited these activities which covered half of Galicia, as can be seen from the archives of the Association, which have luckily been preserved.

In the 19th century, the youth press was born, though publications were short-lived. Among the earlies were the satirical Wesz (Louse), 1835 and Świstek (Scrap of Paper), 1848. Later on, the Ognisko (Focus) became an important journal (1889).

The period of the Springtime of Nations

During the "Juvenalia" at the end of the academic year, students dress up in medieval costume and make merry

The students' choir in medieval costumes leaving the Collegium Maius for the Jubilee celebrations in 1964

(1848) saw hectic activity among political youth organizations. A National Guard was formed in Cracow, and meetings were held at which students protested against professors who showed excessive loyalty. The students sent a delegation to Vienna and obtained the release of political prisoners. As a result of one of the protest meetings, Professor Józef Maciej Brodowicz, whose attitude was markedly pro-Austrian, was forced to resign his chair. This activity was considered premature or not properly prepared and, as a rule, met with opposition on the part of the professors; yet it did help to consolidate the Polish character of the University.

The students' song and dance ensembles often in bizzare costumes like to gather in the courtyard of the Collegium Maius to perform the so-called beani, i.e. jocular scenes poking fun at freshmen

In the 1850's the Students' Reading Room was established. It existed for nearly 70 years (until 1923) as a youth organization and generally maintained a radical attitude, especially towards the end of the 19th century, when notions of progress, of work among the masses, of socialism and independence, penetrated to Cracow from the Russian-occupied part of Poland. The work of the Reading Room caused a great many discussions and even altercations with the Academic Senate, and local government authorities, and even with the Ministry in Vienna. After 1905, the Reading Room became a mainstay of the peasant movement.

Beside the Reading Room, there also developed the Fraternal Aid Society which existed until 1939. As the University expanded, such tasks as the running of students' hostels and cheap canteens grew too complex to be managed by students themselves. The same applies to the Medical Students' Fraternal Aid Society. Among the students' mutual aid organizations, mention should be made of the Law Students' Library (established in 1851), an important organization, connected with the University but with a house of its own.

Towards the end of the 19th century, a number of scientific societies were founded, including the Historians' and Geographers' Circle (1886), the Philologists' Circle (1879) and the Aestheticians Circle (1891). A special position was held by the Academic Choir (from 1878). This time also saw the expansion of regional youth organizations grouping for instance students from Tarnów, from Silesia or from the Podhale region, etc., and also of other associations like the friends of Classical Drama or literary societies (such as the "Helion"). Nor should the Students' Sports Union (AZS) be overlooked. It is impossible, however, to list all associations, their number was immense and though some were ephemeral, others existed for several decades. Only a few (the Academic Choir and the Sports Union for instance) have survived to the present day.

From the middle of the 17th century, public meetings of students became an established custom. As a rule, they were long and tempestuous. If convened with the Rector's consent, they were held at first in the courtyard of the Collegium Maius or of the Nowodworski College and later (after 1890) in the vestibule and staircase or the Copernicus Room of the Collegium Novum. One of the most important functions of these meetings, especially in the 1860's, were appeals for the complete Polonization of the University; a prominent leader of this movement was Alfred Szczepański.

The police did not interfere with meetings held within University precints. Sometimes, however, meetings were held outside the University, in restaurants or hotels and those occasionally ended in disturbances. In 1890, students smashed the bust of Rector Korczyński in the First Clinic of Internal Medicine in Copernicus Street, demanding the Rector's resignation. Disputes, agitation and demonstrations intensified in the last years of the 19th century when socialist ideas spread to Cracow. The professors who failed to understand the essence and the deeper causes of this great social unheaval, tried to oppose and hinder it but on the whole to no avail.

Student meetings were announced by special handwritten or hectographed leaflets. One such leaflet, announcing a meeting in the courtyard of the Jagiellonian Library, has been preserved and we reproduce its text: "Fellow Students! At our insistent request, Mr. W.(incenty) L. (utosławski) has agreed to expound before the students of the Jagiellonian University his views on the proper way of celebrating national anniversaries, today, 29 November 1900. We shall assemble at 3 p.m. in the courtyard of the Jagiellonian Library in St. Anne's Street, and all students are invited to attend this meeting, and to refrain from any vociferous demonstrations which would be improper on so solemn a day.*) We shall hear W.L. in a quiet and solemn atmosphere and then we shall disperse without provoking any scuffle that would detract from the importance and dignity of the celebration. The participation of more mature secondary-school pupils and of girl-students from the Baraniecki courses would be welcome."

The chief organizers of this meeting were Florian Sobieniowski (later to become a well-known author and translator of George Bernard Show and Bogusław Serwin (later an artist).

In 1890, demonstrations took place in connection with measures taken against the Students' Reading Room. The two interwar decades saw strikes and protests, including the famous "blockade" or sit-in strike organized by progressive left-wing youth in the first students' hostel in 1937. On the eve of World War I, students engaged in hectic campaigns for independence and other civic causes. This activity and the influence of the younger generation on the course of events in World War I is well known. On 31 October 1918, students took a massive part in the liberation of Cracow from Austrian rule.

---

*) 29 November was the anniversary of the outbreak of the November Uprising of 1830.

First-year students assembled in the courtyard of Collegium Maius for the inauguration of the academic year 1968/69

After World War I, youth organizations (Roman Catholic, rightist, socialist and communist, peasant, Ukrainian or Jewish) clashed in sharp debates and even fights. Each organization had its Curator appointed by the Senate; his task was to see to it that University regulations and the statutes of the organizations were not violated. There was quite a considerable amount of trouble and friction and in many cases the University Senate failed to understand new currents and tendencies. In spite of all the difficulties, however, the activities of students' organizations had, on the whole, beneficial results. Among the youth leaders of those times, quite a few were to hold high positions in the Polish People's Republic after the 2nd World War; they have retained warm and vivid memories of the years of their early activities.

The Second World War and the terrible

Nazi occupation strengthened the ties between youth organizations and the University. As in the rest of Poland, the alumni of Cracow's higher schools in those years became the mainstay of both underground education and political and civic activity.

Much historical information on student life and activities is contained in collective studies on this subject, published in Cracow in 1964. It should also be noted here that an association of alumni was formed on the occasion of the University's 600th anniversary. This organizes congresses and meetings which enjoy great popularity.


## HIGHER EDUCATION FOR WOMEN

Another novelty, and a truly revolutionary one, was the admission of women to the University and, later on, the gradual appearance of women as professors and heads of various University institutes. In the 19th century, women were not admitted to the University, with the exception of the medical faculty which ran midwifery courses at the surgical clinic. In the 1860-s, along with final-year medical students (37 in all), women were also admitted to attend lectures in obstetrics; there were 20 such students who studied midwifery for two years. Every morning, the professor inspected the clinic, accompanied by students of both sexes.

Meanwhile, the first women doctors appeared in Western Europe and in America and Polish women went abroad to study more and more frequently (e.g. Maria Skłodowska-Curie). It hardly does credit to the Jagiellonian University that, in defiance of realities, it resisted women students for so long. It illustrates the provincialism of the University in the 19th century and the shortsightedness of many professors. Eventually, however, higher education for women became a fact in Cracow around 1900.

Towards the end of the 19th century courses for women were started by Dr Adrian Baraniecki, a distinguished physician and civic leader, at a time when the University gates were still closed to women. The lecturers at the courses were, for the most part, University professors.

After 1900, the Baraniecki courses gradually lost importance.

In 1894, the Academic Senate was confronted with a difficult problem. Three young women from Warsaw (i.e. from the Russian-occupied part of Poland) who had already gone through a practical training in pharmacy applied for admission to the department of pharmaceutics. The opinions of the professors were divided, but since women were already studying in Switzerland, France and America, and it was considered desirable to exert a certain influence on the Russian-occupied part of the country, where Polish schools did not exist, the applicants were allowed to enroll. Their graduation two years later was a true sensation.

The Jagiellonian University students' register of 1900 shows that there were 26 women students and 229 men in the Philosophical Faculty, which at that time comprised both the humanities and natural sciences. The relatively low number of women students is due to the fact that

The oldest woman graduate of the Jagiellonian University (enrolment year 1897) visits the Collegium Maius occasionally to relive memories of her younger days

there were no girls' secondary schools teaching classics, which was required for university entry.

At first, women studied mainly arts subject. Most of the students used their family names without the suffix "-ówna" used by single women. With every passing year, the number of women students grew by several dozen, so that on the eve of World War I, their number was almost equal to that of men.

In 1919, women were at last admitted to the law faculty, the last (apart from theology, of course) to open its doors to women. The first woman professor was Mme Helena Wilman Grabowska, who was appointed in 1923 to the chair of Sanscrit in the Department of Philosophy.

All over the world famous universities receive many distinguished foreign visitors. The Collegium Maius is visited every year by several thousand prominent personalities, including royalty, leading statesmen, scientists and representatives of the arts. All sign their names in the visitors' book

*Collegium Maius* # Collections

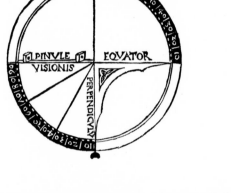

HOW DO THE COLLECTIONS OF THE JAGIELLONIAN UNIVERSITY
• COMPARE TO SIMILAR UNIVERSITY COLLECTIONS ABROAD ? •
THE UNIVERSITY'S ATTITUDE TOWARDS ART IN THE 19TH
CENTURY • THE FOUNDATION OF THE UNIVERSITY MUSEUM
IN THE 19TH CENTURY • BENEFACTORS AND DONORS •
FURTHER BEQUESTS • TIMES OF UNREST • THE SECOND
WORLD WAR • PORTRAITS • PAINTINGS • SCULPTURE •
THE GDAŃSK STAIRCASE IN 1949 • THE GOLDSMITH'S ART,
SILVER AND PEWTER • TAPESTRIES AND EMBROIDERIES •
SCIENTIFIC INSTRUMENTS • CURIOSITIES AND MEMENTOS

## HOW DO THE COLLECTIONS OF THE JAGIELLONIAN UNIVERSITY COMPARE TO SIMILAR UNIVERSITY COLLECTIONS ABROAD ?

University museums won approval rather late. Only recently has it come to be acknowledged that a museum of this kind is neither a symptom of collector's mania, nor a result of mere snobbery or vanity, but in fact an important educational aid. University instruction after all has changed its character. Formerly speculative and often theoretical, it has now become empirical, and rational, and requires the student's direct contact with the subject. The history of the discipline studied, the life and work of men who played a leading role in its development, earlier theories and scientific discoveries as well as old methods and instruments all have their place in a university course. More than a hundred years ago for instance, history of medicine became a compulsory subject for medical students and nowadays more and more attention is paid to the history of various other disciplines.

An understanding of scientific traditions encourages the student to become attached to his subject.

The older the school, the richer its history, and the more clearly it is reflected in the University collections.

It would be easy to expand these reflections and turn them into a treatise on the educational role of University museums — a role that is still not always properly appreciated. However, suffice it to say at this point that University museums are often thought to be nothing but repositories of the past (glorious but remote life), or of rare objects illustrating professional ambitions. The situation in this respect has greatly improved but much still remains to be done.

Among the oldest and most important University museums are those of Bologna, Padua and Pavia in Italy. Bologna's Museo Storico della Università is perhaps closest in character to our Cracow collection. In Padua and Pavia old lecture rooms have been preserved ; the collections in Pavia are mainly devoted to the history of medicine and the biological sciences.

In neighbouring countries, one might cite the art collections in the Repin Institute at Leningrad University, the collections of the Institute of Architecture and Art in Moscow and the beautiful interiors and collections of astronomical instruments in the former Poczobut observatory in Vilna, where the Cracow scientist Jan Śniadecki worked for several years. In Prague, a University historical museum is now being established in a 14th-century Collegium, but it is still in the initial phase of organization. In Germany, the University in Münster has an archeological and a geological museum. There are also two University museums in Marburg (of art and history of religion, respectively) and in Heildelberg) archeological and musical collections.

In France, the Revolution and later-on the Napoleonic reforms swept away old traditions and introduced a new spirit in the universities which had no sympathy for museums. In Great Britain, on the other hand, traditions have always been respected and Colleges in Oxford and

Cambridge and St. Andrews in Scotland have collections and old furnishings of great interest and value.

The most famous collections are those of the Ashmolean Museum in Oxford. Unfortunately, this was reorganized a hundred years ago and the old display-cases were lost in the process. Cambridge boasts three excellent University museums devoted to: botany, archeology and ethnography and to the history of science. In America, the oldest University art museum was established in 1832 by Yale University in New Haven, Connecticut. Splendid 300 year-old collections, are to be found in Harvard University which has as many as seven separate museums, the largest being the Fogg Museum. The

One of the finest pieces in the sculpture collection is this statue of the Madonna and Child from the beginning of the 15th century. Its great resemblance to the famous Madonna from Krużlowa, now at the National Museum in Cracow makes it likely that both works come from the atelier of the same master

The former Galenus lectorium now houses the archeological collections of the University Museum

Archeological Museum of the University of Pennsylvania in Philadelphia also deserves mention.

What about Poland? As far as University museums go, we by any means rank last. The Warsaw collections unfortunately were almost totally destroyed or dispersed during the 2nd World War. The University of Warsaw barely managed to save its main library with its valuable Cabinet of Prints. Wrocław is another town that still has old buildings, old traditions and old University mementos.

114

There is no doubt, however, that the position of Cracow is unique. The Jagiellonian University has six scientifically run museums alone, namely, the Museum of the Jagiellonian University in the Collegium Maius (to which this book is devoted), the Zoological Museum, dating from the 18th century, the museums of Geology and Mineralogy dating from the same period, the Anthropological Museum and the Cabinet of Engravings in the Jagiellonian Library. The Museum of the history of Medicine, now transferred to the Medical Academy, remains closely connected with the University (to which it formerly belonged) by the very character of its collections.

Two more University institutions ought to be mentioned here, if only in passing ; in fact each of them deserves a special monograph. One is the Jagiellonian Library, a constantly growing collection of books, inseparably linked with the University and the other — less famous but of the utmost historical importance — is the Archive which for six centuries has preserved diplomas, records of sessions and meetings, inventories and correspondence related to the University.

These University collections, with the possible exception of the Jagiellonian Library, are relatively little known and often not properly appreciated. It is true that they are very modestly endowed and have a very small staff but none the less they grow from year to year and their future prospects are bright.

Heavy wrought-iron door from the beginning of the 16th century with royal eagles. The door belongs to a small wallsafe

As a result of various changes and reconstructions, a new room, the so-called Green Room, was added to the 1st floor of the Collegium's south wing where the professors' lodgings once used to be. It now contains paintings, china and antique furniture. The ceiling is supported by beams from the Cracow Clothiers' Hall; beneath the ceiling runs a replica of a 17th-century painted frieze

Still waiting to be organized into museums are the University's archeological collections and collection of musical instruments. The latter is gradually growing into a separate museum of musical instruments and of mementos of Chopin and Paderewski.

Let us add in conclusion that the term "museum" is an old one and appeared in Cracow as early as the 18th century. At that time, the term denoted a collection of educational equipment rather than a public institution open to visitors.

To sum up it may be said that as far as University museums go, Poland holds one of the foremost places in the world thanks largely to the Cracow collections. Often we do not realize ourselves how very valuable are the collections assembled in the course of centuries within the University walls, thanks to the forethought and devotion of many generations of scholars.

This room of the Commission of National Education contains astronomical instruments once used by Jan Śniadecki and the scientist's portrait

# THE UNIVERSITY'S ATTITUDE TOWARDS ART IN THE 19TH CENTURY

The University has always shown its appreciation for the world of art, although obviously, its approach was different in every century. At the turn of the 17th and 18th century, the professors were responsible for the erection of St. Anne's Church, Poland's finest baroque place of

Displayed in the Room of the Commission of National Education are quadrants, globes and some astronomical instruments as well as paintings from the period. Some of the paintings come from Hugo Kołłątaj's collection

The Karol Olszewski and Władysław Wróblewski corner in the Jagiellonian University Museum. Assembled here are the instruments the two scientists used to liquefy oxygen in 1866

worship, which bears testimony to its founders good taste and expertise. In 1766, the University assumed patronage over the painters' guild and the reformer, Hugo Kołłątaj, himself a collector, repeatedly tried (in 1785, 1806, and 1810) to introduce art studies into the curriculum. In 1778, he brought from Jihlava (Moravia) his friend, the artist Dominik Estreicher (1750—1809) to be drawing-master in Cracow schools associated with the University. At that time, the first lectures in antiquarianism, architecture and material culture were introduced

The physics and chemistry room. Displayed in are old retorts and laboratory glassware

(Jacek Przybylski, Feliks Radwański, Józef Bogucicki).

The idea of establishing a school of fine arts and an art museum in Cracow was raised three times in the 18th century, namely in 1747, 1766 and 1787 (cf. Ossoliński's plan).

In 1809, i.e. as soon as Austrian rule in Cracow came to an end, work was begun on the restoration of the Collegium Maius (Sebastian Sierakowski, Feliks Radwański, Michał Stachowicz), and in 1818, in the period of the Free City of Cracow, plans to start art studies in Cracow materialized with the establishment of the School of Fine Arts, which was later transformed into the Cracow Academy of Fine Arts. Its first professors were Józef Peszke and Józef Brodowski, later joined by Wojciech K. Stattler. It was only natural that in a rather small town, with a population of less than one hundred thousand, the University should play the leading role. Its role was even more important since Cracow was a Free City (until 1846) and the University was governed by Poles. The "tutelar courts" of Austria, Prussia and Russia concluded an alliance aimed chiefly against Poland and the Polish liberation movements. When paintings for the Assembly Hall were commissioned from Stachowicz in 1820, when the school of fine arts was established, when lectures were held on the development of art and culture in old Poland, or monuments of art and architecture were described, the professors had to watch out lest they put their reactionary protectors, especially Metternich and Novosiltsov, on their guard. The latter made use of "domestic" reactionaries such as President Stanisław Wodzicki, General Załuski, the Professor Father Jan Schindler, Professor Józef Maciej Bordowicz, who tormented the University with constant restrictions, scented revolutionary and libertarian ideas everywhere, and stifled every initiative. The plan to found a Society of Friends of Art, conceived in 1822, did not materialize until thirty years later. Wojciech K. Stattler (1800—1884), a distinguished romantic artist and professor of painting at the University, a friend of Mickiewicz and Słowacki and propagator of Messianic ideas, had to work under the most difficult circumstances which soon embittered and dis-

couraged him. And yet Stattler's studio produced several outstanding Polish artists including Władysław Łuszczkiewicz, Andrzej Grabowski, Artur Grottger and, above all, Jan Matejko. The latter did his historical research in the Jagiellonian Library, assisted by Professor Józef Muczkowski and later by Józef Szujski.

Matejko not only acquired broad and

A stained-glass window with the Grieving Christ from the late 15th century

118

Two stained-glass windows from the middle of the 14th century, representing the Holy Family and Christ in the Temple. They probably come from St. Mary's Church in Cracow, where similar windows are to be found

thorough historical knowledge there but also produced his remarkable study on "Costumes in Poland". The artist frequently stressed his indebtedness and gratitude to the University and bequeathed to it the original drawings for "Costumes in Poland", donated several of his works and painted scenes from the history of the University ("Copernicus", "The University in the 15th Century"). In 1886, the University conferred on Matejko an honorary doctor's degree. Even when he was already a famous and widely recognized artist, Matejko would come to hear Professor Marian Sokołowski's lectures on the history of art and sat in the benches together with students.

Like Matejko, Stanisław Wyspiański —

poet, playwright and painter — must be considered a pupil of the Jagiellonian University. He not only studied history of art there but maintained friendly relations with University professors who very early detected and appreciated his talent. They supported and promoted the work of the artists in the "Young Poland" movement by awarding prizes through the Academy of Learning to works which often had not yet won public recognition. This support for art and artists occasionally caused friction and heated discussions, but as a rule, talent and love of art eventually triumphed. In the years 1917—1921, the "Formist" movement aroused great interest in Cracow although there was opposition, too. One of the founders

119

Wall-hangings of the Duke de Crequi in the Rector's staircase. They are in gros-point and probably come from the Royal Manufactory in Paris. They were donated to the University by Franciszek Ksawery Pusłowski

art and in arousing interest in Cracow's historical monuments. They also collaborated with the Art History Commission of the Academy of Learning and with the Society of Friends of Cracow History and Monuments. This gave rise to numerous plans for the preservation of monuments, to discussions, and sometimes protests, on vital matters concerning art and the protection of monuments.

All these matters still remain to be adequately investigated and documented. The Institute of the Art History at the Jagiellonian University played an immense role in the past; its influence reached all over Poland and to neighbouring countries. The collections and scientific material assembled by the Institute in earlier times, although considerably reduced during World War II, still remain a body of great scientific importance. Last but not least, the Institute of the Art history at the Ja-

Two globes from 1541, made by Gerard Mercator, the famous 16th century cartographer

of this movement, the artist Leon Chwistek, became docent in mathematical logic at the University in 1927. Today, the Jagiellonian University Museum owns the largest single collection of his portraits, paintings and water-colours.

The history of art and archeology departments at the Jagiellonian University deserve special attention; Józef Łepkowski first arranged the University collections, his successor Marian Sokołowski initiated modern research in art history, Piotr Bieńkowski devoted himself to classical archeology, and Władysław Demetrykiewicz to prehistoric archeology. All these were thriving disciplines in Cracow. The pupils of these professors (Jerzy Mycielski, Julian Pagaczewski, Feliks Kopera, Tadeusz Szydłowski) played a prominent role in research in the history of Polish

giellonian University has produced many scholars who contributed to the organization of Polish museum and conservation work and their pupils — and now their pupils' pupils — are continuing their great work.

## THE FOUNDATION OF THE UNIVERSITY MUSEUM IN THE 19TH CENTURY

We have already spoken of the early history of the collections in the Collegium Maius. These collections accumulated gradually as a result of the work of many generations; they grew out of various collections since the 15th century when they were started by a set of astronomical instruments of Marcin Bylica from Olkusz, donated in 1492.

In the 19th century, the museum collections in the Collegium Maius became distinctly separated from the library collections. The Museum at that time included excavations, historical objects, scientific instruments, coins (probably Poland's oldest collection), works of art, treasures, and a large collection of professors' portraits.

After 1860, the directorship of the Museums was taken over by Józef Łepkowski, an eminent archeologist and professor of art. Since the Austrian authorities, for political reasons, did not consent to the name "Museum", the collections were called "Art and Archeological Collections". Under Łepkowski's direction it became an autonomous University institution and acquired bequests of valuable works of art, historical relics and national mementos which we shall later describe in greater detail. At that time (1886—1940), the Museum was housed in the Collegium Novum and was visited by a great number of groups and foreign guests.

Cracow (like Warsaw and other Polish cities) at that time had no museums since the occupying Powers treated suspiciously anything that roused the national consciousness of the Polish people. It may by recalled in this connection that the celebration of the 500th anniversary of the University (in 1864) was restricted or, to be more precise, stifled by the authorities in Vienna. Warsaw's Central School (University) was dying as a result of harassment and restrictions. Under these circumstances, Józef Łepkowski's efforts to build a University Museum, set the collections in order and find funds and

The exhibition of astronomical instruments occupies one of the rooms on the 1st floor. In the foreground are old telescopes

donors, must be acknowledged as a work of immense devotion and persistence, worth examining more closely.

## BENEFACTORS AND DONORS

The benefactors of the University are those who contributed to its growth, whether by bestowing gifts of value, land or money, or by bounding chairs and institutes. Among the benefactors were kings, famous personalities, artists and statesmen — but also modest citizens who wished to show their attachment to the

University and to science by any gift, however small.

In this outline of the history of the Jagiellonian University Museum, we deem it necessary to cite the most important

from about 1470, two superb Augsburg tankards and silver plates from Sigismund III's pantry, a fine ivory bas-relief with the effigy of Sobieski; snuff boxes

Christ Teaching in the Temple — painted in 1614 by the Venetian artist Vincento Amati. It shows a view of Jerusalem and the portico of Solomon's Temple supported by spiral columns

it necessary to cite the most important donors who contributed in the 19th century to the growth of the art collections of the University and, by their donations ensured that, in spite of all the ravages and calamities that have afflicted the University, its Museum still has one of Poland's most valuable collections.

Edward Rastawiecki (1805—1874) deserves to come first. He was the author of a Dictionary of Polish Artists (published in 1857) and, in connection with this work, paid frequent visits to Cracow to collect material. He was a friend of Łepkowski and donated his collections "to the illustrious Alma Mater, to become part of her Archeological Collection". They were of a diversified character, including documents, casts, seals, artistic handicrafts, above all examples of the goldsmith's art. Among Rastawiecki's gifts are a Marshal's baton with golden ferrule, one of the finest specimens by Dresden goldsmiths

(belonging to Stanislas Augustus and Frederick Augustus), and so-called Przeworsk sashes from the 16th century. The Rastawiecki collection replenished the University treasury, impoverished by the catastrophe of the partition.

Rastawiecki's gifts also included a silver sugar-bowl and inkstand, several wine goblets, as well as ivory sceptres. Although the latter bear the ciphers and portraits of Polish kings, they are in fact 19th-century imitations made by Dresden goldsmiths, who counted on the interest of Polish collectors. Some of these items, for instance a large silver tray with an unidentified battle scene, are of artistic value in spite of their inauthenticity.

Aleksander Przeździecki (1814—1871), historian, publisher of source material and art expert, was a close friend of Rastawiecki. He deserves great credit as the editor of the works of Długosz. Łepkowski acted as secretary in this publishing

Ladislas the White, a Piast prince of Gniewkowo, was the nephew of King Ladislas Łokietek and a claimant to the Polish throne. Impetuous and irascible, he quarrelled with Casimir the Great. He roamed across Europe as a knight errant, became a Cistercian monk, later a Benedictine, and finally landed in prison in Dijon. This suited Louis of Hungary who succeeded Casimir the Great to the Polish throne. In this beautiful painting, Jan Matejko shows the Piast prince in a heroic pose, musing over his vicissitudes

Edward Rastawiecki and Konstanty Przeździecki were among the outstanding benefactors of the Jagiellonian University in the second half of the 19th century. Rastawiecki was the author of a "Dictionary of Polish Painters" and a collector of archeological relics. Przeździecki founded a valuable library in Warsaw, and also edited the works of Długosz. Both bequeathed their collections to the Jagiellonian University Museum

project, and thus the Museum received several dozen sets of Długosz's complete works, donated by Aleksander's son, Konstanty. For many years (until 1939), the Museum derived profits from the sale of these books.

Konstanty Przeździecki also donated his father's collection of Polish excavations, "considering it an honour that Aleksander Przeździecki's collection should be kept in Poland's greatest institution". In 1894, Konstanty Przeździecki purchased and turned over to the University and to its Institute of Art History, the library of Józef Łepkowski, after the latter's death. It contained valuable inventory notes, drawings and water-colours (including a portfolio relating to the renovation of of royal tombs in the Wawel Cathedral). Another part of Łepkowski's manuscripts (notes concerning historical weapons, notes for a catalogue of Poland's historical monuments, and personal correspondence) went to the Przeździecki Library in Warsaw, where it was unfortunately destroyed during World War II.

In the history of Polish museums, Wła-

dysław Czartoryski (1828—1894), distinguished himself above all as the organizer of the Czartoryski Museum in Cracow, where the Hôtel Lambert collections from Paris were eventually transferred in 1878. His friendship with Łepkowski accounted for the fact that in 1872 Władysław Czartoryski donated to the University a superb collection of antiquities. It included Cyprian ceramics (40 objects in all, some of them dating from the 2nd millennium B.C.), two Mycenaean bowls, and several dozen items of Hellenic ceramics — jugs, vases, amphorae and pateras. The gift also included ancient lamps, bronze objects or fragments, and very valuable archaic terracotta figurines. The Czartoryski collection contained a total of about 250 items.

The example set by Władysław Czartoryski stimulated others. Within the next few years, further antiquities were donated by Marceli Czartoryski, Justynian Kornecki and Jan Matejko. In this way, a collection of antiquities was started in Cracow.

Karol Rogawski (1819—1889), after a revolutionary youth, settled in 1846 on his estate of Ołpiny near Biecz, and devoted himself to archeological research (Leżajsk and Siedliszowce) and to collecting. As he was a consummate expert and collector, his bequest constituted a most valuable addition to the University possessions. It was greatly diversified and its most valuable part was the collection of painting which included some outstanding work of the Venetian school (Titian, Tintoretto, Tiepolo) as well as other Italian and Flemish schools. Another masterpiece is the portrait of an unidentified man by J. Kupetzky, a Czech-Austrian representative of the Rembrandtiant school. Kupetzky's patron in Rome was Prince Aleksander Sobieski, hence the artist's ties with Poland.

The Rogawski collections also include sculptures, for instance the Pietà (around 1590), the Last Judgment (around 1590), a bas-relief representing St. Jerome (around 1600), ivory objects, tapestries and goldsmith's work. Because of the outstanding value of many items the Rogawski collection ensured the predominantly artistic character of the University collections towards the end of the 19th century, while the antiquities receded into the background.

This list of principal donors should also include the name of Franciszek Ksawery Pusłowski (1874—1967), owner of a palace in Cracow filled with works of art. In 1950, Pusłowski turned over his collections to the Jagiellonian University, although he himself lived in very straitened circumstances. In return, the University looked after its venerable benefactor during the last years of his life. The Pusłowski collection contains national mementos, royal coats of arms, portraits (including a self-portrait by Rubens), sculptures, paintings, and seven superb French tapestries from the middle of the 17th century, embroidered for the Duke de Crequi, Marshal of France.

## FURTHER BEQUESTS

We could not possibly list all the donors who contributed to the Museum in the second half of the 19th century, chiefly in Łepkowski's lifetime. Gifts came from all over Poland. The major donors mentioned above were joined by such institutions as the Cracow Friends of the Fine Arts, the Poznań Friends of Learning, the Academy of Learning in Cracow, the Cracow Academy of Fine Arts, as well as by private persons (W. Kuncewicz, T. Żebrawski, J. I. Kraszewski, W. Kretkowski, E. Zieliński, J. N. Sadowski, B. Biskupski, J. Polkowski, J. Lasocki) whose gifts doubled the collection of coins. In 1894, the Jagiellonian Library turned over to the University Museum a collection of numismatics and seal casts. This is Poland's oldest numismatic collection and dates back to the 16th century (Stanisław Grzebski's bequest).

Łepkowski's energy and enthusiasm produced effects. Gifts poured in from the Smithsonian Institution in far-away Washington as well as from Russia (coins donated by T. Hlushaninova); Henryk Bukowski, the well-known antique dealer from Stockholm and benefactor of many Polish collections, sent to the Museum translations of runic inscriptions. Wojciech Lanna from Prague donated catalogues of engravings (1896), and E. Włodkowicz sent many photographs and reproductions which were later turned over to the Institute of Art History.

It seems fitting to recall certain other gifts: in 1874, Wiktor Czajewski offered sculptures from the predella of the altar at Kleczków; in 1876, Albina Brunicka from Lwów donated an agate spoon which, according to tradition, had belonged to the Empress Eleonore; according to other sources, the spoon had been made by Sigismund III. Around 1800, the University received from A. Mieleszko-Maliszkiewicz a ring with the following Arabic inscription engraved on a semiprecious stone: "Among all men, there is none equal to Mohammed". Tradition has it that this ring was captured in the battle of Vienna, together with other treasures belonging to the Grand Visier. In 1887, Adam Wiszniewski from Turin sent from Paris a portrait of his great-uncle, Antoni Wiszniewski, the distinguished Piarist educator, and a marble bust of his father, Professor Michał Wiszniewski, literary historian of literature. In 1889, Gustaw Okołowicz from Warsaw donated a faience plate from the Belvedere manufactory, dated 1776. In 1896,

Majolica flower-vase of Florentine workmanship, from the middle of the 15th century. On the front is a heart pierced with an arrow, and the inscription "Margerita"

Tile (mid 17th c.) with the "Nałęcz" blazon of Piotr Gembicki, bishop of Cracow. All that remains of a stove which stood in the Cracow bishops' palace until the mid 19th century

Countess M. Apraksimova from Russia gave the caparison that her grandfather, General Rakhmanov, had taken off the horse on which Prince Józef Poniatowski died in the waters of the Elster river (1813).

Long is the list of donors. In 1900, on the occasion of the 500th anniversary of the University's revival, the people of the Greater Poland province gave to the Rector a large saphire ring, and the people of Vilna a Rector's mace. At the same time, M. Potulicka sent to the University a silverplated table which was said to have belonged to King John III.

The University sometimes received quite unexpected gifts from the most unexpected people.*) In 1933, a modest working man from New York named Jagiełło (which perhaps accounts for his feeling fellowship with the University) bequeathed a large sum of money to the University.

When Ignacy Paderewski's last will was made known in 1941, it turned out rather unexpectedly that he had left nearly all his estate to the Jagiellonian University although he hat not been a frequent visitor to Cracow and had studied elsewhere. He must, however, have appreciated the honorary degree conferred upon him by the University. Recently, an American of Polish descent, Czesław Dziadulewicz, a lawyer from Milwaukee, bequeathed to the Collegium Maius valuable publications on museology. On the occasion of its 600 anniversary celebrations, the University received several splendid gifts, among them a gold medal from the University of Ferrara. Other recent additions to the treasury include a collection of old clocks

---

*) With no offence meant to any of the distinguished benefactors of the University, men of famous names and outstanding merit, one can hardly fail to mention the humblest donor, of a discernible profession, to whom nonetheless gratitude is due: in 1967, the Criminal Court remitted to the University a bronze medal, some sixty years old. The medal was found "on a professional thief, already sentenced many a times. He could not explain how the said object had come into his possession. When the defendant learned that the object would be confiscated, he requested that the medal, which he valued highly, be turned over as a memento to the Jagiellonian University — which is hereby being done"

from Okno, bequeathed by Professor T. Milewski, several Oriental rugs donated by Professor T. Piotrowicz, and a valuable 15th-century parchment sheet with

and to Canon Mariampolski in the 18th century, to the above-mentioned generous donors in the 19th century, and to present-day donors. In many cases, wars and

Statuette of Augustus III, made in Meissen porcelain (around 1760), probably by J. J. Kaendler, and two Delf vases, from the middle of the 18th century

miniatures, a gift of Professor T. Wierzejski, a well-known collector from Warsaw.

One more comment. The reader may wonder why we write so much about the various donors. Many of them died a long time ago and have no living descendants today. Why then ?

The answer is : out of gratitude and to fulfill our — the museum's — part of the bargain.

In the past, benefactors of the University requested that the provenance of their gifts be clearly marked. The University promised to do so to Professor Benedykt from Koźmin and to Abbot Jan Ponętowski in the 16th century, to Primate Andrzej Olszowski in the 17th century, to Professor Stemplowski and Bogucicki

removals, have unfortunately obliterated the original arrangement and composition of the collections. Besides, times have changed and so have museum requirements. Yet, the memory of the donors can always be preserved by means of appropriate plaques, information in catalogues or the display of their portraits as is practiced in the Collegium Maius.

TIMES OF UNREST

It is a tradition of the University to look after its treasures and to safeguard them in case of danger. Even if in peacetime some worthy professors have not shown enough care for the University collections, in times of war and unrest there was always someone who made sure that the insignia, mementos and works of art were hidden in a safe place.

As early as the 15th century, documents and inventories refer to the prohibition of lending or pawning University treasures. The inventories show that a regular check was kept on the contents of the University treasury which were obviously highly valued.

The danger that threatened the treasury during the siege and occupation of Cracow by the Sweden in 1655, was averted by removing the insignia to far-away Vienna, from whence they did not return until a few years later.

In 1794, in the critical days of the Kościuszko Insurrection, the University gave away its jewels, silvertable ware, liturgical vessels, rings and gold coins. The relevant records read :

Inventory of gold and silver issued by the treasury of the Cracow Academy, on the orders of the Supreme Commander of the national armed forces, to S. Dembowski and S. Mieroszewski, Commissioners delegated by the Public Order Commission of the Voivodship of Cracow, on the 13th day of May 1794.

"Gold : primo, gold chain of an estimated value of 528 Polish zlotys, secundo, rings, a small chain and other small objects of an estimated total value of 126 Polish zlotys.

"Silver : primo, Jakub Piotrowski's large wine-goblet with lid, all gilded ; secundo, large wine-goblet with the Leliwa and Odrowąż coats of arms, with lids ; tertio, two large goblets, folding, with the Srzeniawa coat of arms, all gilded ; quarto, large goblet without lid, with forged base, all gilded ; quinto, two large goblets, matching, with lids, all gilded ; sexto, Doctor Bernard's large goblet with lid, all gilded ; septimo, large goblet with icicle pattern ; octavo, three-legged bowl, with lid, all gilded ...

"Remaining are : primo, three Academic maces, one of them large, all gilded ; secundo, two chalices with patenas for the Collegii Jagiellonici chapel. Signed : Rev. Wincenty Smaczniński, Jacek Przybylski.

"The following receipt for the gold and silver received was signed by delegates of the Public Order Commission of the Voivodship of Cracow : We have received from the treasury of the Academy one chain of pure gold, valued at 528 zlotys ; minor gold objects valued at 126 zlotys ; and silver — the standard being noted in the delegates' diary — to a total of 436 grzywnas (marks) and 9 ounces. For the above, the delegates give to the Academy a provisional receipt, to serve as official guaranty of the loan of said valuables to the national treasury, and they refer the lenders to their Commission. On the thirteenth of May, 1794, at the Major Jagiellonian College : S. Dembowski and S. Mieroszewski, manu propria."

The University also gave to the insurgents a considerable proportion of its surveying instruments, which were needed by the artillery, as well as gold coins. The maces were kept in consideration of their historical value and were concealed in the countryside, near Żywiec. Jan Śniadecki also repurchased at that time the gold chain donated by Jagiełło's sister, Princess Aleksandra and, since he could not return it to the University (which was then under Austrian rule), he donated it to the Czartoryski collections at Puławy. The Czartoryskis returned the chain to the University in 1927.

At the beginning of the 20th century, it might have seemed that the University collections were safe, but even the First World War proved a serious threat to museum on Polish territory. The University jewellery survived World War I, hidden in the basement of the National Bank. When, in 1920, a thief broke into the Rector's office, he took away only 19th-century silver-plated chains. All the same the insignia were not properly safeguarded.

As a result of the reorganization of many institutions, and the establishment of new Universities and new collections in Poland, the suggestion — unfortunate to say the least — was put forward in the years 1921 and 1922, to abolish the Jagiellonian University Museum and to distribute its collections among various other Polish museums. The University opposed this, of course, just as it had always opposed even the loan of its treasures to anyone. It is worth recalling at this point that in 1900 the University refused to lend maces to an exhibition of art of the Jagiellonian era (which caused much resentment), and in 1915 it declined the request of its Rector, Stanisław Tarnowski, the donor of two portraits by Matejko, to lend these portraits to an exhibition in Vienna; and this in spite of the fact that Tarnowski's request was supported by court circles in Austria. It must be admitted that Tarnowski accepted the decision of his colleagues with true magnanimity.

## THE SECOND WORLD WAR

The years of the Second World War were the hardest in the entire history of the Collegium Maius, Library and Archives. The Collegium Maius was deserted. Shortly before the war, the new building of the Jagiellonian Library had been completed in Mickiewicza Avenue, and at the very outset of the occupation the entire University Library was quickly transferred to its new premises.

The Nazi occupying forces showed their usual rapaciousness with regard to the University treasures. The majority were assembled in the basements of the Academy of Mining and Metallurgy, where the office of the Governor-General was located, and were drawn upon at will. At first, works of art were removed for what purported to be official purposes; then the wives of Nazi notables took their pick of valuable objects that were irretrievably lost; finally many precious relics were seized as gifts for dignitaries, above all for Hitler, Frank, and Goering. The brothers Kai and Joseph Mühlmann, historians of art from Salzburg, did the greatest damage, followed by Professor Dagobert Frey from Vienna, the architects E. Horstman and F. Koettgen from Hamburg, and the conservator Dr. Werner Kudlich from Vienna. The arrest of 184 Cracow professors on 6 November 1939, became a signal for a massive attack on the University collection. Without further ado the Mühlmanns and Kudlich proceeded to remove what they liked. On 17 May 1940, for instance, Kudlich took away a widely known drawing by Wit Stwosz, which according to later depositions, was given to Hitler in his headquarters in Prussia.

The Jagiellonian University Museum suffered grievous losses. Of the Persian rugs,

only three survived. Also lost, among other things, were a painting by Wouvermann, Wit Stwosz's letters to the city council of Nuremberg, many valuables including Limoges enamels, engravings, mementos, and artistic handicrafts.

The insignia fortunately survived in the hiding place that had been prepared for them a few months before the war in the cellars of the Collegium Novum. On 1 September 1939, Professor Adam Bochnak took the maces from the Rector's office and bricked them up so well in the underground cache that they remained there safely until the liberation.

In the years 1940—1944, whatever had escaped being looted, was hidden in nooks and crannies of Cracow's libraries, or in a deserted synagogue, in the stores of the National Museum, in the botanical gardens, in the attics of University colleges. This accounts for the fact that many paintings, portraits and pieces of furniture were saved.

Also saved, eventually, were the objects which were removed to Bavaria. While destroying the Jagiellonian University as a major centre of Polish learning and culture (*Bastion des Polentums*), the Nazis intended to establish in its place an Institute of German Science in the East. For this purpose, they took over the Collegium Maius and began to assemble there objects from former University collections. When the Soviet army was approaching Cracow, the entire Ost-Institut was hastily evacuated to the castle of Zandt, in Bavaria. The collections hidden there were traced and recovered. In May 1946 about ten rail-car loads returned to Cracow and to the Collegium Maius.

In subsequent twenty years, the Jagiellonian University Museum was slowly brought back to life and even entered a period of new splendour, thanks to its fine setting in the restored Collegium Maius.

## PORTRAITS

The time has now come to have a look at some works of art. Let us start our review with the gallery of paintings in the Collegium Maius. There are of course

Sigismund III Vasa and his wife, Anna of Austria, portrayed around 1592. The two portraits are valuable examples of Cracow art from the end of the 16th century

valuable paintings in other buildings (the Collegium Novum) which will also be dealt with. Among these paintings, the majority are portraits.

Our portrait gallery is not Poland's oldest — precedence must be given to the gallery of episcopal portraits at the Franciscan Monastery in Cracow — but it is probably the richest. The custom of painting portraits took root in Poland in the 16th century, although earlier examples are also known. In the Age of Humanism and Renaissance, it became the fashion to collect portraits of scholars, as well as those of monarchs and magnates. Among the earliest Renaissance portraits in Poland is that of Benedykt of Koźmin (around 1540), a superb specimen of the school of Basel; it shows the learned humanist in his study against a ground of flowers. The inscription (added later)

reads: "This is Benedykt of Koźmin who enriched thee, oh library, both with moneys and books". Several other excellent portraits from the 16th century are of Sigismund III, of Professor Jakub Górski, of Bishop Jan Dantyszek, and of other persons not connected with the University such as Caterina Cornaro, Queen of Cyprus (Tintoretto? Veronese?) and Benvenuto Cellini (school of Titian). It should be added, for the sake of accuracy, that the University did not acquire the latter two portraits until the 19th century.

In the 17th century, the collection of portraits of kings, professors and other personalities connected with the University, grew considerably. The University commissioned royal portraits and displayed them in its Assembly Hall, thus stressing their role as patrons. Tomaso Dolabella, Marcin Kober, Jan Trycjusz, and other

Cracow artists painted portraits of professors in gowns, with learned books at their side or inscriptions extolling their knowledge and merits. Portraits of bishops were also painted, partly of necessity since they were Chancellors of the University, although this patronage often brought more trouble than profit, especially in the 17th century.

Paritcularly noteworthy is the fact that in the 17th century Professor Jan Brożek commissioned for the Library in the Collegium Maius portraits of Copernicus and his father. At the same time, the University had portraits of Jadwiga and Jagiełło painted twice (for the Assembly Hall and for the Library), as well as a portrait of John Sobieski (by Jan Trycjusz).

In the 18th century, new portraits were added to the gallery. Among the best is that of Rector Żołędziowski, made in Rome by Tadeusz Konicz. New acquisitions include also the official portraits of King Stanislas Augustus and of his brother, Primate Michał Poniatowski (who

Portrait of Hetman Jan Tarnowski by M. Bacciarelli (c. 1790). Formerly believed to be a copy, it is now recognized as a replica made by the artist

This portrait of Marcin Kromer (1512—1589) is one of the oldest University portraits and shows the historian in bishop's robes. Kromer's *Polish Chronicles* was one of the most popular of late medieval historical works

initiated the reform of the University), as well as numerous portraits of Rectors.

The University remained faithful to the portrait tradition in the 19th century. A nephew of Hugo Kołłątaj for instance, gave to the University a fine portrait of his uncle. It was in fact usual for the portrait of a professor to be offered to the University by his family or friends. Acquired in this way were portraits of

131

Józef Dietl and Józef Szujski by Matejko. Stanisław Tarnowski gave his own portraits, also by Matejko. The University also received several portraits by Kazimierz Pochwalski, Julian Fałat, Leon Wyczółkowski and Jacek Malczewski.

Today the portrait gallery of the University includes more than four hundred works, for the most part displayed in various rooms of the Collegium Maius. All the more distinguished professors are represented there.

## PAINTINGS

The collection of paintings is also of considerable interest. Related to the history of the University is the so-called foundation painting (known to us from a copy only) which at one time hung above Jagiełło's tomb in the Wawel Cathedral. Around 1620 the University commissioned the artist Tomaso Dolabella to paint a large "Crucifixion" (preserved to this day) in which Jadwiga, Jagiełło and St. John of Kęty are portrayed.

Towards the end of the 18th century, it was decided to embellish the Library

The portrait gallery of the Jagiellonian University ranks among the richest in Poland. It comprises more than 600 portraits of prominent personalities of the world of science and culture. Shown here are a portrait of Professor Jakub Górski, a philologist (middle of the 16th century) and a portrait of the famous goldsmith, Benvenuto Cellini, (attributed to the school of Titian); another epoch is represented by the portrait of Salomea Słowacka-Bécu, mother of the poet Juliusz Słowacki; the portrait of an unidentified nobleman is by the Czech artist J. Kupetzky; the next portrait (similar in style to Paulo Veronese) represents Catherine Cornaro, Queen of Cyprus; next there is a portrait of Professor Marcin Gilewski (1571) and one of Stanislas Augustus in the uniform of the Knights' School, soon after his accession to the throne; the next portrait, by F. Szynalewski, represents Alojzy Estreicher, Rector of the Jagiellonian University in 1831; the last portrait, of interest for the history of printing in Poland, represents Franciszek Cezary, court printer and librarian in 1651

Three portraits: the writer Zenon Parvi by S. Wyspiański, Kazimierz Kostanecki, professor of anatomy by L. Wyczółkowski, and a self-portrait by the artist Olga Boznańska

rooms with paintings showing scenes from Polish history. The artist Franciszek Smuglewicz was even commissioned to do this work which was not, however, carried out. It was not until a quarter of a century later that — as was mentioned previously — the artist Michał Stachowicz decorated the Jagiellonian Room with mural paintings depicting scenes from the history of the University.

Through the organization of the museum by Professor Łepkowski and the various bequests the University acquired what could be properly called an art gallery. The collection contains today about two hundred excellent works, from medieval to modern paintings, including some by Italian and Flemish masters. Several works by Polish artists, including Matejko, Wyspiański, Malczewski (the "Legends" series), landscapes by Wyczółkowski and Fałat, water-colours by Leon Chwistek, complete this varied collection. The Jagiellonian University Museum also owns several very valuable sets of graphics, such as drawings by Szymon Czechowicz and Franciszek Smuglewicz and sketches by Moniuszko, Matejko, Wyspiański, Jerzy Mehoffer.

Closely connected with the section of engravings, is the collection of about three thousand woodcut blocks, one of the richest of its kind in the world, which originated in Cracow's printing-houses in the 16th-18th centuries.

## SCULPTURE

The sculpture collection in the Collegium Maius is as well endowed as the portrait and painting galleries. Of great interest are the foundation plaques i.e. bas-reliefs in stone, commemorating the construction of a building. Among the most impressive is the plaque of the Jerusalem dormitory, founded by Cardinal Zbigniew Oleśnicki in 1452. The plaque from the house of the famous humanist Erazmus Ciołek (originally in Kanonicza Street) dates from the transition period between the late Middle Ages and early Renaissance (1505).

In 1891, Józef Mehoffer and Stanisław Wyspiański designed a stained-glass window, composed of several panels, for St. Mary's Church in Cracow. Here is one of the panels representing The Dormition

PROJ. S. WYSPIAŃSKI.
WYKONAŁ
KRAKOWSKI ZAKŁAD WITRAŻÓW S. G. ŻELEŃSKI.

The Annunciation (c. 1500) is a tomb painting of a knight who is shown kneeling by his coat of arms, the "Jastrzębiec". In spite of subsequent repaintings, it is a good sample of Cracow art of the late 15th century

The Judgment of Paris is an interesting example of Polish art of the first half of the 17th century, devoted to mythological themes. The painting gives the impression of being an illustration of a theatrical performance

The Jerusalem dormitory, it is interesting to recall, stood until 1836 near the Collegium Maius, in Gołębia Street, on the present site of the Collegium Novum. Legend has it that Oleśnicki's foundation was connected with his unfulfilled vows to make a pilgrimage to Christ's tomb. The bas-relief shows the Cardinal kneeling before the Madonna on her throne and offering her a model of the student dormitory. Oleśnicki's portrait is a remarkable likeness and the whole plaque attests to the high standards of Cracow's

Artur Grottger's painting "The Three Fates Unreeling the Thread of Life" is actually a portrait of three 19th-century belles, after the fashion of the 2nd Empire period in France. Grottger probably made this painting during his stay in Vienna

Girl with Pigeons, by Adrian Frans Boudewyns, a Dutch artist from the second half of the 17th century

Medor and Angelica inscribing their names on a tree-trunk — Venetian painting from the mid 18th century, probably by Gianbattista Tiepolo

The Szczerbrzusz Madonna, time- and weather-beaten after long years in a roadside chapel, dates from about 1420

This Pietà is one of the most valuable works of medieval sculpture in the Collegium. It dates from around 1480 and probably comes from the Austrian Tirol

A statuette of Casimir the Great from the end of the 14th century. A copy of it is displayed in the place of honour in the oriel-window of the Common Room. In the background is a 16th-century Persian rug

scultptors, although its author remains unknown. The style is earlier than that represented a generation later, around 1480.

The collection of medieval wooden sculptures opens with an interesting, although modest, wooden reading-desk, supported by an eagle. This comes from a Rhineland workshop of the early 14th century. From the same period (and, perhaps from the same area) comes a figure of the Madonna and Child.

Of particular value for the history of Polish art is a small figure of the Madonna and Child dating from the first years of the 15th century which is very close to the famous Madonna from Krużlowa, now in Cracow's National Museum. A comparison of the two works, of the arrangement of the drapery, the angle of the

Plaque commemorating the foundation of the Jerusalem dormitory in 1453. Of particular interest to us is the kneeling figure of Cardinal Zbigniew Oleśnicki, holding a model of the dormitory. Oleśnicki's face, executed with great realism, resembles his other portraits. The artist unfortunately remains unknown, but probably was a Cracow sculptor

Four works of medieval art: Madonna and Child (13th-century), the expressive Prandocin Madonna (c. 1380), the Madonna of Good Hope (c. 1420) and St. John the Baptist (c. 1460)

Madonna and Child, from the foundation plaque of the Jerusalem dormitory (1453)

body and, finally, of the mood suggested by the two sculptures, brings us to the inescapable conclusion that both come from the same workshop. This again makes it highly likely that the Madonna from Krużlowa is not an importation from abroad but a local work, probably from the Cracow region.

St. Anne with the Madonna and Child — a sculpture from the circle of Wit Stwosz (c. 1500)

Two figures of Christ: Christ Resurrected (c. 1460) and Grieving Christ (c. 1470)

The Pietà from the late 15th century, on the other hand, is not a Polish but an Austrian work of art, and distinctly resembles sculptures of this type in the Austrian Tirol. It is of great artistic value, all the more precious because our museums do not have many foreign works of medieval art.

141

Two kneeling Angels with candlesticks — a sculpture from the end of the 14th century. The Angels are wearing blue robes and long red cloaks with thick folds

Putta playing with a buck — 18th-century bas-relief by the French sculptor M. Falconet

Modesty — sculpture in bronze by the great French artist J. A. Houdon (18th century). Donated to the Museum by Franciszek Ksawery Pusłowski

Heraldic plaque of Bishop Erasmus Ciołek (1505) — a sample of early Renaissance sculpture. Above the crest held by two angels is the figure of the infant Moses in his basket, an obvious allusion to plebeian origin

Hercules Strangling the Serpent, an extremely valuable Florentine sculpture from the beginning of the 16th century (c. 1510). In the 18th century highly prized as a work of the young Michelangelo

## THE GDAŃSK STAIRCASE IN 1949

During the renovation of the Collegium Maius, a carved oak spiral staircase made in Gdańsk around 1700, was installed in the Common Room, opposite the windows. The staircase dates from a period when carpentry flourished in Gdańsk, Elbląg and other towns of Pomerania. It consists of a central shaft around which wind spiral stairs with a carved handrail. Next to the staircase is a landing and the entrance is guarded by the figures of two knights in pseudo-Roman costume. The staircase was part of the furnishings of a house (no longer standing in St. John's Street in Gdańsk). Around 1880, they were bought in Gdańsk and transferred to a palace at Krzeszowice, where they remained until 1946, though damaged by the effects of time and war. This is not the only piece of Gdańsk carpentry in the possession of the University.

It is true that very little has been preserved of the old furnishings of the Collegium's halls and rooms. As was mentioned earlier, the Collegium Maius was taken over in the 19th century by the Jagiellonian Library which had its own requirements as far as the interior outlay was concerned. The furniture which we see today comes either from 19th-century donors or has been acquired recently or reconstructed on the basis of surviving elements. This applies in particular to the heavy oak stalls in the Assembly Hall, modelled after the pews in St. Anne's Church.

As regards 19th-century furniture, changes in taste fortunately allow us to appreciate this nowadays. In the rooms once occupied by professors, for instance we find armchairs from Gen. Chłopicki's drawing-room, chests of drawers, tables, chairs and a bed belonging to Ambroży Grabowski, historian of Cracow and librarian, and a musicbox once belonging to the Siedlecki family. If we keep in mind the great devastation in Poland (and especially in Warsaw) of interiors a hundred years old or more, these modest furnishings preserved in the Collegium Maius, coming for the most part from professors' families, acquire a special lustre for us.

The Jagiellonian University Museum owns and collects old museum display

The superb staircase in the Common Room, made in Gdańsk at the turn of the 17th and 18th centuries. The steps and richly carved handrail wind around a spiral stem. Standing on guard at the foot of the stairs are figures of fantastic halberdiers

furniture. Formerly, this was done partly of necessity, because museum cabinets and show-cases are, as a rule, quite expensive. Nowadays, they are collected in full awareness of their historical value.

The door leading to the "Lord's Room" of the former Cracow Town Hall was given to the University collections in 1836. It is a sample of late-Renaissance Cracow woodwork (c. 1600) which shows Dutch influence

Among the oldest are vestry cabinets from the middle of the 18th century, from St. Anne's University Church, which are now placed in the Libraria. Exactly alike or very similar are the archival and library cabinets, purchased for the Collegium Maius in 1766. Also of interest are the large show-cases and tables acquired

by Kołłątaj in 1810, when he bought for the University Professor Hacket's natural history collections (Their show-cases were designed by Sebastian Sierakowski). The Museum also owns laboratory benches from around 1840 and glazed cabinets from the years 1860—1870, not to mention museum furnishings from more recent times.

## THE GOLDSMITH'S ART

Examples of the goldsmith's art form a separate section of the museum. As was mentioned earlier, many objects were given away for the needs of the Kościuszko Insurrection, and on the whole only the maces and small insignia were kept back. The 19th-century maces, used for routine ceremonies, are now kept in the Rector's office in the Collegium Novum. Insignia of artistic and historical importance are kept in the treasury of the Collegium Maius.

Outstanding among examples of the gold-

Pewter plate and jug from the middle of the 16th century, Nuremberg work

The Collegium Maius treasury includes valuable examples of the goldsmith's art. It also possesses a collection of pewter vessels displayed in the Common Room. Here are Renaissance goblets from the 16th century, a Nuremberg tankard and a pewter tray, plate and mug

Wrought-iron decoration on the gate of the Collegium Maius in St. Anne's Street. An example of 17th-century Cracow work. The traditional motifs of fantastic coils, bird's beaks and animals derive from the Middle Ages

This small bronze mortar from 1646 was used for experiments in physics, alchemy, pharmacy and chemistry

smith's art are two silver tankards from the 16th century, a silver box set with rhinestones, a rich collection of 16th-century spoons, including an Italian agate spoon (probably from Cellini's atelier),

plates from the 16th century and two snuff boxes of unusual beauty — one the property of King Stanislas Augustus, the other of Frederick Augustus, Duke of Warsaw.

Monstrance base of gilded copper from the beginning of the 15th century

The grate from Cracow's former Town Hall (c. 1500) consists of two parts : the grate proper, of twigs and rosettes, is in a distinctly late-Gothic style ; the ornamentation of the door imitates a pattern of dry branches

The treasury rooms are separated by a 17th century iron grate

Mention should also be made of the superb anointing crown from the 16th century (of unknown origin, probably a North-Italian product) and a multitude of minor valuable objects and mementoes from more recent times (an inkstand belonging to Stanisław Koźmian, and a plate owned by Ignacy Paderewski, etc.).

SILVER AND PEWTER

Until the end of the 18th century, table-settings were relatively modest. Earthenware bowls, ornamented to a greater or lesser degree were in general use and in the countryside, wooden vessels prevailed. Silver dishes or cuttery were a rarity. As last wills and inventories show, even the wealthier professors in most cases left behind silver, spoons and tumblers only.

The Jagiellonian University Museum has a fine collection of spoons beginning from the 16th century when forks were not yet widely used. These spoons bear various inscriptions such as "Save me, dear Lord, in Thee I trust", "For a piece of silver,

Gothic brass plate with a figure of a woman holding a wreath donated, according to an obscure tradition, to the Jagiellonian University by Callimachus; plate with Annunciation scene is from the 15th century; the plate of Queen Constance, wife of Sigismund III is from the end of the 16th century

Silver tankard from Gdańsk (c. 1600) decorated with silver thalers and effigies of Polish king Stephen Batory, Sigismund III and John-Casimir; tip of baton decorated in gold; pewter oil-lamp

a rascal is hanged", "In every matter, mind your honour", "Great lords also fall". Some silver vessels bore the names, coats of arms or other signs of their owners.

The richest collection is that of pewter objects. Pewter plates and cups were in use since the middle of the 17th century. The Museum has pewter plates of various shapes and makes; most come from Silesia but there are also some from Cracow. In the Common Room, the shelf over the wainscotting has a fine display of pewter plates and jugs. Mention should also be made here of the rich collection of copper cake-moulds, which to our knowledge are extremely rare in Poland.

Persian rug from the beginning of the 17th century woven with silver and silk threads, an example of what are known as "Polish" rugs. It is said to have been donated by John III after the victory of Vienna in 1683

Burgundian tapestry from the mid 15th century showing the sleeping Noah being ridiculed by his son Ham, whose name in Polish has become the epitome of rudeness. Unfortunately this is all that remains of a larger composition depicting the whole story of Noah

## TAPESTRIES AND EMBROIDERIES

The University has a rich collection of tapestries, beginning with ancient Coptic hangings from Egypt (c. 1st-3rd centuries). The collection of tapestries is above all, an indispensable teaching-aid, since a knowledge of tapestries is necessary to every historian of art and museologist, to every designer of costumes or textiles.

149

have preserved all their original splendour. Today, these tapestries hang in the "Rector's staircase" by which prominent guests are ushered into the Assembly Hall.

The University also owns three early 17th c. Persian rugs, woven with silver and gold thread. Rugs of this kind were made in the Shah's weaving shop. One was given to the University by Sobieski

In 1951, Franciszek Ksawery Pusłowski, lecturer in foreign languages at the Jagiellonian University, donated to the Museum part of his priceless collection, inherited from his ancestors. It included a series of gros-point tapestries embroidered for the French Marshal de Crequi (around 1687). The tapestries have retained all the brilliance of silk embroidery. They probably come from Louis XIV's manufactory in Paris and were designed by Le Brune. At the same time, the University received from Pusłowski a superb Louis XIV tapestry, said to come from Versailles and representing the triumphal chariot of the Sun King. The details of this tapestry, which truly deserves to adorn a monarch's palace, indicate a designer and manufactory of the highest class

The most valuable items owned by the museum are a set of seven silk-embroidered hangings, representing elements and symbols as well as the coat of arms of the Duc de Crequi, Marshal of France. These hangings are not Gobelins but were made in grospoint embroidery and were probably designed around 1670 by the great French artist Charles Le Brun who was the director of Louis XIV's artistic manufactories. The superb colours

after the victory of Vienna, the others he gave to St. Mary's Church in Cracow, from which the University later obtained them. As was mentioned earlier, out of the original seven rugs, only three were saved, the other four were taken away by the Nazis.

Also noteworthy among the tapestries is the fine French Gobelin with the coats of arms of France and Navarra, (the royal coat of arms of Louis XIV). This Gobelin, in bronze and gold tones, represents the king's chariot and the emblems of his power, his victories and rights.

## SCIENTIFIC INSTRUMENTS

So far we have dealt mainly with the Jagiellonian University's art collections, although this is only one side of the museum's work. The other side is concerned with the equally valuable collection of scientific objects.

Almost everything in this rich and varied collection comes from various University laboratories or institutes, but was only assembled during the last few years. The display of astronomical, physical and chemical equipment has recently been enlarged by biological specimens and instruments.

Let us begin with the oldest instruments. The bequest of Marcin Bylica of Olkusz (around 1492), mentioned here several times, consists of a celestial globe connected with an astrolabe, a torquetum for the measurement of stellar angles, and astrolabes of which the oldest, an Arabic one, dates from the 11th century. Alongside these instruments, mention should be made of a small globe known as the "Jagiellonian", famous because it bears the inscription "America noviter reperta". A larger copy of this globe is kept in "Polish Room" of the University of Pittsburgh, in the United States.

The collection of astronomical instruments also includes telescopes and quadrants etc. from the 17th and 18th centuries which, together with 19th-century instruments, provide an interesting survey of the history of astronomy. These instruments are exhibited in an 18th century room, named after the National Commission of Education and connected mainly

Arabian astrolabe from 1156, the University's oldest astronomical instrument

The so-called Jagiellonian Globe is a small, very precise clock, with a globe inside and an armillary sphere (c. 1510). On the globe the American continent is marked. The inscriptions read: "America noviter reperta" and "Terra Brezil". A copy made in 1937 is at the University of Pittsburgh, Pennsylvania

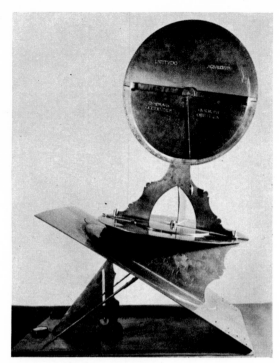

The turquetum of Marcin Bylica of Olkusz, court astronomer in Hungary, bequeathed to the Jagiellonian University in 1492

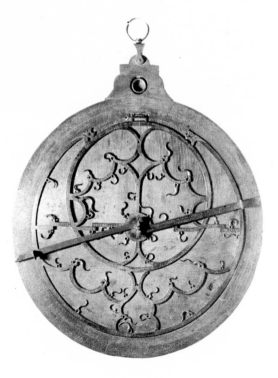

The astrolabe of Marcin Bylica of Olkusz (1486)

with the person and work of the Polish mathematician Professor Jan Śniadecki. The instruments are for the most part very decorative and to the contemporary observer seem to be an ideal demonstration of the relationship that can exist be-

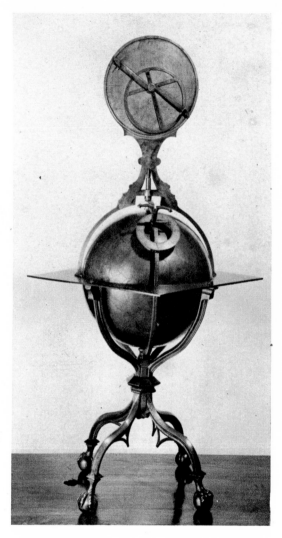

This 15th-century celestial globe also belonged to Marcin Bylica. The astrolabe was added to it later, around 1480. The globe served above all for astrological purposes

tween a work of art and a work of technology. We are delighted by the beauty of the quadrants struck by the contemporary form of the armillary spheres with their abstract design of interlocking circles and fascinated by the large heavy

153

clock, a product of the blacksmith's art of the 15th century, which moves like a living creature!

Let us return to the astronomical instruments, whose provenance in some cases is well known. In Śniadecki's letters for instance, we read of the efforts to obtain a telescope from the English firm of Dollond (still existing in London today). Thanks to Stanislas Augustus' assistance, a Canivet quadrant was brought from Paris and a Ramsdey telescope from England. When we inspect these objects today, we find it difficult to believe that in Poland, devastated by so many wars,

Equatorial sun-dial from the middle of the 18th century; ring-shaped sun-dial and surveying instrument from the middle of the 17th century

This armillary sphere, marking the course of the stars, was made in the middle of the 17th century by Professor F. Słupski, teacher of Kołłątaj

instruments from the Age of Enlightenment have been preserved in good condition as a material link with those years of the Constitution of 3 May (1791).

There are so many instruments that we cannot name them all. A model of an Archimedes' screw comes from the 17th

Early 19th century sun-dial cube with a compass in its base, and a pocket sun-dial with compass

154

The shank, "cock" and bridge from the carriage clock of P. J. Ris, Cracow clock-maker from the middle of the 18th century. The mechanism of a tower-clock from the end of the 15th century, probably made in Cracow according to the manual of the Italian master-mechanic and clock-maker Dondi

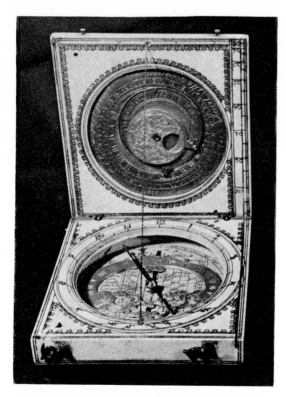

Exceptionally beautiful pocket sun-dial in an ivory box, made in Dieppe, France, in the 18th century

Small telescope bought by the astronomer Jan Śniadecki from the London firm of Dollond, in 1792

century, the glass vessel for chemical distillation, known as Pelican, dates from the 16th century and probably served for experiments in alchemy in which certain

Sextant made by E. Lenoire in Paris (around 1780), used by Napoleon during the Egyptian campaign

professors at the University secretly engaged.

Father Andrzej Trzciński, a physicist, brought from Paris a Nollet vacuum pump, an instrument made with Rococo elegance. The same Trzciński, a rather difficult man to get on with, but a distinguished scientist, conducted the first research in electricity in Cracow. It is to him that credit is due for the presence in the collections of the earliest electrical machinery and appliances such as Wolf bottles, a Pixie magneto-electrical machine, a Volta pistol, galvanometers and intensifiers.

Almost every branch of modern technology and of the natural sciences in Poland is represented in the Jagiellonian Uni-

The terrestrial globe (1599) and celestial globe (1603), which have adorned the library room in the Collegium Maius since the 17th century, were made by Wilhelm Blaeu. Marked near the southern polar circle is the Terra Australis Magellani. The two globes rank among the most valuable objects of this kind

versity Museum. Let us just mention a 19th-century magic lantern, Warsaw-made calculating machines, a model of a steam engine, a model of water-works, araeometers and anemometers. Among microscopes, two date from the 18th century; one of them, particularly valuable, was the property of Jan Śniadecki.

 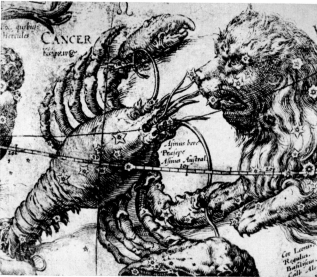

Globes are not only cartographical instruments but often works of art as well. This is especially true of celestial globes which show the constellations in the form of fantastic animals, offered free play to the imagination. Here we see the constellations of Cancer, Leo, Taurus and Perseus, drawn with a wealth of baroque fantasy

Two 16th century alchemists' vessels. The more valuable is the so-called pelican, a vessel for the circulation and distillation of liquids. To our knowledge, this is the only glass vessel of its kind to have been so well preserved

Copper distillation vessels. In front is a 16th century "bulb" which is older than the kettle in the background

157

A "tangent" compass from the 18th century and Magdeburg hemispheres for the investigation of vacuums; two electrical instruments and a 17th century model of an Archimedes screw

Late 18th century Dutch-made microscope; a thermostat used by Olszewski for low temperature research, an anemometer and a heliostat; apothecary's scales from the 19th century

A model of a French water pump from 1840. The model was used at the University for the teaching of mechanics in the middle of the 19th century

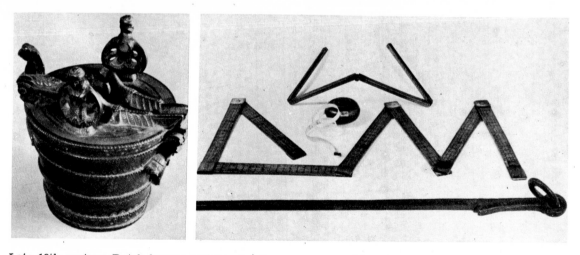

Late 18th century Dutch bronze weight and three measures of length; a medieval bronze ell, a folding rule, surveying tapes and a folding ell

Apparatus constructed in 1884 by Professor K. Olszewski which he used to liquefy oxygen. The apparatus consists of a cylinder, manometer and reservoirs

Let us pass to another epoch, to the period of scientific positivism, of rational and exact research at the end of the 19th century. Preserved intact is the apparatus used by Karol Olszewski and Zygmunt Wróblewski when they liquified oxygen in 1883. Olszewski afterwards continued to do research into the condensation of gases, the separation of the components of air through partial distillation and the investigation of the absorption spectrum of oxygen which brought fame both to him and to the Jagiellonian University. In the 1890's the great Scottish Physical Chemist, Professor William Ramsay, sent Olszewski samples of argon and helium he obtained for the first time.

All these instruments have been preserved to our day in their original shape and were indeed used in lectures untill recently.

A tragic memento has also been preserved. Professor Wróblewski died of burns caused by an overturned kerosene lamp and in commemoration his contemporaries kept the broken lamp, together with the reading-desk at which the accident occurred.

## CURIOSITIES AND MEMENTOS

In 1782, the German author Abraham Penzel attacked Professor Józef Putanowicz, for keeping in the Library of Collegium Maius naive objects which he maintained were a disgrace to the University. Wrote Penzel: "Putanowicz has placed in the library the club with which Cain killed the godfearing Abel, a tooth of St. Christopher which you would swear was a young elephant's tooth, and the horn of a unicorn (monocerotis) which I have ascertained to belong to a fish. He also has a code which he believed to be Jason's lost book — and he had good old Appian's name included in the list of theological authors... Good Lord, if I had a hundred mouths, they still would not suffice to tell about all those objects in which the famous librarian Putanowicz chose to see things quite different from what I would or could see in them...".

This attack by Penzel, which greatly damaged the reputation of the Jagiellonian Library and of its collections, has not been critically reviewed to this day and is still being quoted as evidence of the University's medievalism. Actually, however, what Penzel and others after him ridiculed were in fact so-called curiosities — "raritates", — collected in Cracow as in any other major institution of learning in the 16th and 17th centuries. Similar collections existed at the same time in Rome (Museo Kirchiano), in Oxford (The Ash-

molean), in Vienna, and in Leyden. Very few of these collections have survived, those which still exist, however, are highly valued by historians of science and culture. The University acted in keeping with the collecting theories of their time. The heads of the Library were probably influenced by such theoretical works as M. Valentino's "Museum Museorum" (1714) or J.K. Neikel's "Museographia" (1724), the latter being particularly close to us as it was published in Leipzig and Wrocław.

Part of these University curiosities (which we know from inventories) have survived in spite of all adversities. Some keep re-emerging in University collections, in the various institutes of natural sciences or humanities (the "horn of the unicorn" for instance, which turned out to be part of Cardinal Bernard Maciejowski's verge). Still to be seen are the fossils, as well as what purported to be Sarmatian bronze skeletons but which actually are anatomical models; then there are Hercules strangling the serpent — a superb marble sculpture from the 16th century, and various coins, medals, seals, etc. Other exhibits are now kept in the Anatomy Institute of the Medical Academy, or in the Museum of the History of Medicine;

Golden snuff-box with a diamond monograph of Frederick-Augustus, Duke of Warsaw and King of Saxony (1810)

Golden snuff-box belonging to Stanislas Augustus with his miniature. Probably made in Dresden, around 1780

Empire clock belonging to Hugo Kołłątaj, made by D. Estreicher and offered to Kołłątaj in 1807, after his release from prison in Olmütz

pathy. Along with works of art and scientific instruments, the Jagiellonian University Museum also has such a collection of mementos of famous men, which are a vital token of our attachment to the illustrous personalities of the past.

Apart from the Copernicana, mentioned earlier, the oldest mementos include the University insignia. The oldest mace is connected with the Jagiellonian restoration of the University in 1400 and the Rector's chain is a gift of Princess Alexandra of Mazovia. Royal mementos also include the clock of Sigismund Augustus (or, perhaps of Sigismund III ?).

It could hardly be possible to enumerate all the mementos, such as the astronomical instruments of Professor Jan Brożek, the instruments of Jan Śniadecki (microscope and telescopes), or items owned by Kołłątaj (carriage clock).

In memory of Stanislas Augustus, the University has a silver spoon, a lacquer tray, and a snuff box which was his own gift. In memory of Kościuszko — it possesses his old Virtuti Militari orders and of Prince Józef Poniatowski — his pistols and the caparison of the horse on which he lost his life.

Mementos from the 19th century are more numerous. There is a coffer for papers and an inkstand belonging to Joachim Lelewel and Jacek Malczewski's palette. Stanisław Wyspiański is represented by the quill (he never used any other pens) with which he wrote his drama "Acropolis". A peculiar exhibit are two cigars which Mickiewicz and Odyniec lighted from the hot lava on Vesuvius in 1830.

Tragical mementos from the period of the Second World War when Cracow professors were detained in the Sachsenhausen-Oranienburg concentration camp (1939—1940) include notebooks, a hat, an urn, pieces of clothing, letters and photographs.

some curiosities are also kept in the collections of the various clinics. It is a task for the future to put together again, if only in some publication, what has been inconsiderately dispersed ; this could be set right if the present keepers of the various objects showed more understanding for the cause of the reconstruction of our collections.

The passion for preserving mementos of famous people and of historic events is one with which most people are in sym-

# HISTORIOGRAPHY

The Jagiellonian University has played so important a role in the history of the Polish culture that the historical literature on it is immense. It begins in the 17th century with works by S. Starowolski and M. Radymiński. In the 18th century, J. A. Putanowicz and A. Żołędziowski wrote about the University and in the beginning of the 19th century J. Śniadecki, H. Kołłątaj and J. Sołtykowicz made their contribution. Each of these authors viewed the University's past in his own way. Later-on, Jerzy Samuel Bandtkie and Józef Muczkowski, and then nearly all Cracow historians (in the broadest sense of the term) considered it their duty to write at least a single chapter of the University's history, to discuss at least a single episode in its long story. Sources were also published, including charters, statutes, records of Rector's courts, conclusions reached at sessions and student registers.

In 1900, Kazimierz Morawski, although a classical philologist (Poland's last excellent Latin orator), published his monumental *History of the Jagiellonian University in the 15th Century*. At the same time, Father Jan Fijałek wrote a monograph on Professor Jakub of Paradyż, the 15th century Cracow philosopher and theologist. While Morawski demonstrated how close had been the University ties in the 15th century to State and religion, Fijałek stressed that at the time of the Ecumenical Councils, the University, together with the Paris Sorbonne, had fought for conciliarism within the Church.

Research into the history of the University entered a new phase in the two decades between the First and Second World War. The most important work published at that time (1935) was Henryk Barycz's "History of the Jagiellonian University in the Age of Humanism". With the appearance of this work, research into the history of the University became comprehensive and many-sided ; it extended into modern and contemporary history and dealt not only with science and scholars, but also with youth organizations and political ideas.

A collective *History of the Jagiellonian University* (Cracow 1963—1964), as well as numerous monographic studies were published on the eve of the 600th anniversary celebrations.

In many works on the history of the University there is a clear tendency to seek symptoms of its future decline as early as the 15th century. This reflects a kind of impatience towards the subject and towards people, an inclination to acknowledge only great efforts and impressive achievements, a sort of inferiority complex in relation to the achievements of other centres of learning. Even so great a scholar as Aleksander Brückner (in his *History of Polish Culture*) snarls again and again at the University. He fails to see it against the background of Poland's calamities and struggles and only demands greatness of Cracow professors.

The opinion on the decline of the University in the 17th and 18th centuries was established by its great reformer, Hugo

Portal with the inscription „Ne cedat Academia"

Kołłątaj. A revolutionary innovator himself, Kołłątaj had a tendency to lay all the blame on certain persons or institutions, so as to render the carrying out implementation of his reforms easier. This is what he did with regard to Stanislas Augustus, when he blamed the King for the fall of the Constitution of 3rd May, and this is what he did with regard to the University professors in the period prior to 1778, before the reform, when he gave an exaggerated picture of their low scientific standards. This was an over-simplification for which we may forgive this great statesman and benefactor of Polish education — but which we do not necessarily accept as true. After all, Kołłątaj largely used at the University the same men he criticized so sharply, and could only have done so because they were not steeped so deeply in ignorance as he claimed. Besides, Kołłątaj's closest collaborator and co-author of the reform, Jan Śniadecki, indirectly conceded this by withdrawing, as it were, from his former position.

What is so easily termed the decline of the 17th and 18th centuries, should therefore be viewed as a complex phenomenon. It was not perhaps a period of shining glory, but it did have its bright moments, too.

The 19th century showed that the University had staying-power and that it had survived hard tests. This was an age of great scholars, statesmen and educators. In the 20th century, it was able to help in the creation of new institutions of higher learning in Poland in both 1919 and 1945. During the Second World War, by the heroic death of many professors in the Sachsenhausen camp, by underground struggle and underground instruction, it demonstrated the continuity of the patriotic tradition in the University.

## RELATIONS WITH
## THE ENGLISH-SPEAKING COUNTRIES

It seems worthwhile to devote a separate chapter, albeit a short one, to links between the Jagiellonian University and English-speaking countries. Throughout the centuries, the knowledge of England has been considerable in spite of the distance separating the two countries. The document of restoration of the University in 1400 for instance cites the University of Oxford among the famous institutions of higher learning that Cracow should take as its model, thus showing clear awareness of the important centres of contemporary scholarship.

The first truly significant contact with English thought occurred in the first half of the 15th century when the writings of Wycliffe penetrated to Cracow. Professor Andrzej Gałka of Dobczyn, dean of the a r t i u m faculty, studied the works of the Oxford philosopher, copied them and propagated them with growing enthusiasm. The prevailing theological and ethical trend at the University was conciliarism and this may account for the fact that Wycliffe's adherents were at first treated with forbearance. In 1449, however, reaction set in. Gałka had to flee Cracow and took refuge in Bohemia, where the views of Wycliffe and Huss had numerous followers. In spite of the fact that the University repudiated Gałka's activities (or, perhaps for this very reason), treatises polemicizing with Wycliffe's writings have been preserved in the University library. There are good reasons for believing that the publication (in 1473) of one of the first books to be printed in Poland, namely the *Explanatio in Psalterium* by the Spanish Dominican

Juan de Torquemada, was connected with the fight against Wycliffe and Huss. These matters still remain to be adequately investigated.

An Englishman educated in Oxford who rendered great services to Poland (and who still awaits a special monograph), was the 16th century roving humanist, poet and scholar Leonard Coxe. He first appeared in Cracow in 1519, then he travelled to Hungary and Slovakia and, after five years, turned up again at the University where he began to teach ancient literature. Apart from his official lectures, he spoke to gatherings of youth in the Jerusalem Dormitory where he lived and propagated the works of Erasmus of Rotterdam who counted many Poles among his friends. One of Leonard Coxe's disciples was Jan Łaski, the religious reformer, later well known in western Europe including England. Coxe did much for the study of ancient philology in Cracow and eulogized the University and city in a speech — *De Laudibus Celeberimae Cracoviensis Academiae* — delivered in 1519. In this he sonorously called the city "an Athens full of all virtues", and praised the Cracow humanists, Maciej of Miechów, Paweł of Krosno and Andrzej Krzycki. It was perhaps the new religious ideas that made him leave Cracow and the University which, like most of Poland, supported religious reforms.

We have already mentioned in the chapter on witchcraft practices that in the year 1584 there appeared in Cracow John Dee, astronomer, alchemist and physician rolled into one, who greatly valued his association with the University.

In the 16th century, the tragic fate of Thomas More could not but arouse sympathy in Poland. Preserved in the University is an interesting portrait of More, probably from the second half of the 16th century, attesting to the knowledge, at least, of the events in England.

In the 17th century, in the era of the Counter-Reformation, there was continued interest in England in the University although due to religious differences this was not accompanied by any particular sympathy for the Reformation or the political developments taking place in the British Isles. The manuscript gazettes and reports preserved in the University library, constitute a valuable source of information on this period. Among the most interesting is the "Diplomatic History of Polish-English Relations in the Course of the Centuries" (Ms. 46).

In 1787, the Cracow astronomer Jan Śniadecki went to England where he studied for a year: "y resta un an pur voir etablissement astronomique de ce pais", as he wrote himself in his autobiography. In his letters, Śniadecki described his stay in England, and his collaboration with the astronomers William Herschel and Neville Maskelyn who became his friends. In 1791 and 1792, Śniadecki brought back to Cracow astronomical books and instruments, many of which have been preserved in the Jagiellonian University Museum, (for instance a telescope from the renowned London firm of Dollond's). It is interesting to see reflected in Śniadecki's letters the great respect which the Cracow scholar had for English science.

At the University there were many who were interested in Anglo-Saxon culture. In Śniadecki's times, the knowledge of English literature was propagated in Poland by Professor Jacek Przybylski who published a translation of Milton's *Paradise Lost* in 1791 and compiled biographies and works of English philosophers. From the beginning of the 19th century, the University has offered regular instruction in the English language.

At about the same time, Alojzy Estreicher, Professor of Botany, maintained scientific contacts with the Horticultural Society in London and also corresponded (in 1845) with the collector of meteorites, M. C. Shephard of New Haven, Connecticut.

In the middle of the 19th century, the distinguished philosopher and historian of literature, Michał Wiszniewski, greatly contributed to the knowledge of England in Cracow. In Cracow he published a study on Bacon's philosophy, and in London a psychological study *Sketches and Characters on the Natural History of Human Intellects* (1853).

Wiszniewski was educated in Scotland, at the University of Edinburgh and there established durable bonds of friendship with the poet John Wilson, the philosopher Dugald-Steward, the economist Mac Culloch and the historian Pillans. He also met the novelist Walter Scott, the greatest literary celebrity of the time. In Scotland, Wiszniewski definitively turned away from German speculative metaphysics in which he had formerly been interested. As professor in Cracow he imbued his historical and philosophical works with English rationalism and he inculcated that rationalism in his pupils. Michał Wiszniewski and the English philosophy he taught deserve major credit for the fact that the outlook of Cracow professors in the second half of the 19th century was characterized by moderation, good judgement and rationalism.

In 1886, the two Cracow scientists Zygmunt Wróblewski and Karol Olszewski, were the first to liquify oxygen. In connection with this research Professor Olszewski corresponded and collaborated for many years with Professor William Ramsay, the great British Physical Chemist. Mementos of the friendship between the two scientists are still kept in the University.

In 1900, on the 500th anniversary of the restoration of the University by Jadwiga and Jagiełło, honorary doctor's degrees were conferred on as many as five British scholars: Alfred Marshall the historian, Frederick W. Maitland and the famous physicist Sir John Thompson from Cambridge, and the great surgeon Joseph Lister and Professor William Ramsay from London University. An honorary degree was conferred at the same time on the American astronomer Professor Simon Newcomb from Baltimore. In 1922, the British Foreign Secretary, Arthur Balfour, became an honorary doctor of the Jagiellonian University and, later on, so did Albert Thomas, Director of the International Labour Office in Geneva.

While dealing with English-speaking countries, let us note that honorary degrees were bestowed on two Presidents of the United States — on Woodrow Wilson (in 1918) and on Herbert Hoover (in 1919). In 1964, Professor William Bloom and Linus Pauling were given honorary degrees.

Roman Dyboski (d. 1945) was Poland's first professor of English literature. Actually, he was more than just a teacher of his subject because he also became one of the most active propagators of the culture of English-speaking nations. He wrote much on Shakespeare, and on Anglo-Polish contacts and ties and in the two decades between the First and Second World War travelled several times to England and to the United States, where he lectured on Poland's political problemes.

At that time, German nationalist made exaggerated territorial claims and attempted to convince world opinion that Poland was a country without a culture of her own. Dyboski effectively opposed such claims, and demonstrated how dangerous these chauvinistic theories were. His vivacious oratory, his excellent English and his enthusiasm, commanded wide respect and appreciation. Thanks to Dyboski, many prominent British visitors came to Cracow, for instance the English writer G. K. Chesterton who delivered a most interesting lecture in Cracow in 1929. Roman Dyboski's pupils are still active today in Cracow as well as in America and Great Britain (L. Krzyżanowski, Z. Grabowski).

It was in the same period that Dr William Rose from Canada, later professor at the London School of Slavonic Studies, author of several very important scholarly English works on Poland, graduated in Cracow in Polish philology. He was not only a historian of education but also distinguished for his work as organizer of homes for young people. Professor Rose always remembered his Cracow Alma Mater. This is what he wrote of his studies in Cracow in a fine retrospective essay (1964):

"It is true I was the first man from the English-speaking world to attain the Doctorate in a Polish university in modern times... As for the University, it was in the forefront of European thought in the middle of the sixteenth century; and from 1867, it has marched with the best. In history and literature, in mathematics and both physical and biological sciences, in law and medicine, in the fields of psychology and sociology, it has kept the flag of action and progress always flying..."

The great ethnologist Bronisław Malinowski, professor at London and Yale Universities (d. 1942), was closely connected with Cracow and the Jagiellonian University. It was there that he was educated, obtained his doctor's degree and published his first scientific work on totemism in 1914.

For many years, English was taught in Cracow by M. Dziewicki, a British philologist of Polish origin who, in the 1920's, translated into English the works of Władysław Reymont, Polish novelist and winner of the Nobel prize in literature.

Translated by:
Jan Aleksandrowicz

Reviewers:
Józef Lepiarczyk and Władysław Tomkiewicz

Layout:
Leon Urbański

Editor:
Ewa Muszyńska

Technical Editor:
Maciej Cholerzyński

This is the one thousand three hundred and third publication of Interpress Publishers

Printed in Poland

Photographs by:
E. Czapliński (colour) page 2, 9, 12 × 2, 13, 14, 15, 16 × 2, 17 × 2, 18, 22 × 2, 23, 24, 25 × 2, 26 × 5, 27, 31 × 2, 32, 37, 39, 40, 41, 43 × 2, 46, 50 × 2, 51, 52, 53, 54 × 3, 56, 57 × 2, 58, 62, 63 × 2, 64, 65, 66, 67 (colour), 68, 69 × 2, 70 (colour), 72, 74 (colour), 76, 79 (colour), 82, 84, 93 × 2, 94, 98 × 2, 99, 102, 114 (colour), 115, 115 (colour), 116 × 2, 117 × 3, 118 (colour), 119 × 2 (colour), 120 × 2, 121, 122, 124 × 2, 126 × 2 (colour), 127 × 2 (colour), 130 × 2 (colour), 131, 131 (colour), 132 × 3, 133 × 2, 134, 135 (colour), 136, 137, 138 × 2, 138 (colour), 139 × 2 (colour), 140 × 4, 141 × 3, 142 × 2, 142 (colour), 143, 145, 146 × 2, 147 × 2, 148 × 3, 150 × 3, 151 × 2, 152, 153, 154 × 3, 155 × 4, 156 × 3, 157 × 3, 158 × 5, 159, 162;

From the collections of the Museum of the Jagiellonian University:
Wł. Gumuła: p. 44 × 2, 45, 46, 48, 149, 152, 153;
E. Hartwig: p. 80;

A. Iszczuk: p. 29, 62;
Klinowski: p. 10;
St. Kolowca: p. 46, 47, 48, 61, 75, 96;
A. Krzyżanowski: p. 68;
J. Lewicki: p. 102;
St. Mucha: p. 58, 100;
Pawlikowski: p. 140;
W. Pawłowski: p. 109;
W. Plewiński: p. 100;
B. Pomykało: p. 105, 106, 107;
K. Pomykało: p. 19, 103 × 2;
J. Rosner: p. 73;
E. Węglowski: p. 81, 103 × 2;
pages: 10 × 3, 11, 13, 14, 18, 21 × 2, 23, 28, 30, 38, 39, 40, 41, 43, 44, 45, 48, 51, 55, 59 × 2, 60 × 2, 62, 63, 64, 65, 70, 71 × 2, 72, 73 × 2, 76 × 2, 77 × 2, 78 × 5, 79, 81, 83, 84, 85 × 2, 86, 87 × 3, 90, 91 × 4, 94 × 2, 95, 97, 105, 108, 114, 132 × 2, 133 × 2, 134 × 2, 137, 140, 141, 143, 144, 145, 146 × 2, 147, 148 × 3, 149, 153, 157, 159 × 2, 160, 161 × 2.